Essential

Cantonese

phrase book

Compiled by

Philip Yungkin Lee

PERIPLUS

Published by Periplus Editions (HK) Ltd.

Copyright © 2003 Periplus Editions

ISBN: 0-7946-0154-5

Printed in Singapore

Distributed by:

Asia Pacific
Berkeley Books Pte Ltd
130 Joo Seng Road, #06-01/03
Singapore 368357
Tel: (65) 6280 1330
Fax: (65) 6280 6290
Email: inquiries@periplus.com.sg

Japan
Tuttle Publishing
Yaekari Bldg., 3F
5-4-12 Osaki Shinagawa-ku,
Tokyo 141-0032
Japan
Tel: (03) 5437 0171
Fax: (03) 5437 0755
Email: tuttle-sales@gol.com

North America
Tuttle Publishing
Airport Industrial Park
364 Innovation Drive
North Clarendon, VT 05759-9436
USA
Tel: (802) 773 8930
Fax: (802) 773 6993
Email: info@tuttlepublishing.com

Indonesia
PT Java Books Indonesia
Jl. Kelapa Gading Kirana
Blok A14 No. 17
Jakarta 14240
Indonesia
Tel: (62-21) 451 5351
Fax: (62-21) 453 4987
Email: cs@javabooks.co.id

08 07 06 05 04 03
 6   5   4   3   2   1

Contents

Introduction 5

Pronunciation guide 6

1 Useful lists 9-20

1.1 Today or tomorrow? 10
1.2 Legal holidays 11
1.3 What time is it? 12
1.4 One, two, three... 14
1.5 The weather 17
1.6 Here, there... 18
1.7 What does that sign say? 19
1.8 Personal details 20

2 Courtesies 21-27

2.1 Greetings 22
2.2 How to ask a question 23
2.3 How to reply 25
2.4 Thank you 25
2.5 Sorry 26
2.6 What do you think? 26

3 Conversation 28-37

3.1 I beg your pardon? 29
3.2 Introductions 29
3.3 Starting/ending a conversation 32
3.4 Congratulations and condolences 32
3.5 A chat about the weather 33
3.6 Hobbies 33
3.7 Being the host(ess) 33
3.8 Invitations 34
3.9 Paying a compliment 35
3.10 Intimate comments/ questions 35

3.11 Arrangements 36
3.12 Saying good-bye 37

4 Eating out 38-47

4.1 On arrival 39
4.2 Ordering 40
4.3 The bill 42
4.4 Complaints 43
4.5 Paying a compliment 43
4.6 Requests 44
4.7 Drinks 45
4.8 Cantonese yamcha 46
4.9 Cantonese dishes 47
4.10 Western dishes 47

5 On the road 48-59

5.1 Asking for directions 49
5.2 Luggage 50
5.3 Traffic signs 51
5.4 The car 51
    The parts of a car 52-53
5.5 The gas station 54
5.6 Breakdown and repairs 54
5.7 The bicycle/moped 58
    The parts of a bicycle 56-57
5.8 Renting a bicycle/ moped 58
5.9 Hitchhiking 59

6 Public transportation 60-67

6.1 In general 61
6.2 Questions to passengers 62
6.3 Tickets 63
6.4 Information 63
6.5 Airplanes 65

6.6	**L**ong-distance trains	65
6.7	**T**axis	66

7   **Overnight accommodation 68-75**

7.1	**G**eneral	69
7.2	**B**ooking	70
7.3	**C**hecking the room	71
7.4	**R**equests	72
7.5	**C**omplaints	75
7.6	**D**eparture	76

8   **Money matters 76-79**

8.1	**B**anks	77
8.2	**S**ettling the bill	78

9   **Mail and telephone 80-84**

9.1	**M**ail	81
9.2	**T**elephone	82

10   **Shopping 85-92**

10.1	**S**hopping conversations	86
10.2	**F**ood	88
10.3	**C**lothing and shoes	88
10.4	**P**hotographs and video	90
10.5	**A**t the hairdresser's	91

11   **At the Tourist Information Center 94-98**

11.1	**P**laces of interest	94

11.2	**G**oing out	96
11.3	**R**eserving tickets	97

12   **Entertainment 99-104**

12.1	**S**porting questions	100
12.2	**B**y the waterfront	100
12.3	**S**ightseeing	102
12.4	**N**ightlife	103
12.5	**C**ultural performances	103

13   **Sickness 105-112**

13.1	**C**all (get) the doctor	106
13.2	**P**atient's ailments	106
13.3	**T**he consultation	107
13.4	**M**edication and prescriptions	110
13.5	**A**t the dentist's	111

14   **In trouble 113-118**

14.1	**A**sking for help	114
14.2	**L**oss	115
14.3	**A**ccidents	115
14.4	**T**heft	116
14.5	**M**issing person	116
14.6	**T**he police	117

15   **Word list 119-155**

Basic grammar	**156–160**

Introduction

● **Welcome to the Periplus Essential Phrase Books series, covering the world's most popular languages and containing everything you'd expect from a comprehensive language series. They're concise, accessible, and easy to understand, and you'll find them indispensable on your trip abroad.**

Each guide is divided into 15 themed sections and starts with a pronunciation table that explains the phonetic pronunciation for all the words and phrases you'll need to know for your trip. At the back of the book is an extensive word list and grammar guide that will help you construct basic sentences in your chosen language.

Throughout the book you'll come across colored boxes with a 🗨 beside them. These are designed to help you if you can't understand what your listeners are saying to you. Hand the book over to them and encourage them to point to the appropriate answer to the question you are asking.

Other colored boxes in the book —this time without the symbol—give alphabetical listings of themed words with their English translations beside them.

For extra clarity, we have put all English words and phrases in **black** and foreign language terms in **red**.

This phrase book covers all subjects you are likely to come across during the course of your visit, from reserving a room for the night to ordering food and drink at a restaurant and what to do if your car breaks down or you lose your traveler's checks and money. With over 2,000 commonly used words and essential phrases at your fingertips, you can rest assured that you will be able to get by in all situations, so let the Essential Phrase Book become your passport to a secure and enjoyable trip!

Pronunciation Guide

The Yale System of Romanization

The system used in this dictionary to write Cantonese Chinese with Roman letters is the *Yale* system which is the most widely used system in Cantonese language books and dictionaries. The imitated pronunciation should be read as if it were English, bearing in mind the following main points:

Consonants

b, ch, d, f, g, h, j, k, l, m, n, p, s, t, w, y as in English

ng	like English **ng** in 'si**ng**'
gw	like the English name '**Gw**endolyn'
kw	like English '**Gw**endolyn' with a strong puff of air

Vowels

a	like English **u** in 'f**u**rr'
a(a)	like English **a** in 'f**a**ther'. This long vowel is normally written **aa**. However, it is written **a** when it is used by itself without a consonant (except **h** which is used as a tone indicator for 4th, 5th and 6th tones).
e	like English **e** in 't**e**n'
i	like English **ee** in 'f**ee**'
o	like English **o** in 'h**o**t'
u	like English **oo** in 'f**oo**l'
eu	like English **e** in 'h**e**r' with rounded lips
yu	like French **ü**. In English is pronounced like 'j**ee**p' with lips rounded and pushed out.

Tones

A tone is a variation in pitch by which a syllable can be pronounced. In Cantonese, a variation of pitch or tone changes the meaning of the word. There are six tones: 1st tone is indicated by a horizontal tone mark; 2nd tone is indicated by a rising tone mark; 3rd tone does not carry a tone mark; 4th tone is indicated by a falling tone mark along with the letter 'h' placed at the end of a vowel or group of vowels; 5th tone is indicated by a rising tone mark along with the letter 'h' placed at the end of a vowel or group of vowels; 6th tone is indicated by the letter 'h' placed at the end of a vowel or group of vowels. Tone marks are placed on the first vowel of a final.

Below is a tone chart which describes tones using the 5-degree notation. It divides the range of pitches from lowest (1) to highest (5).

Tone chart

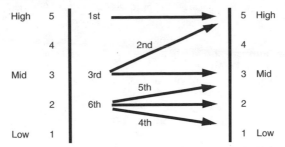

High	5	1st		5	High
	4	2nd		4	
Mid	3	3rd		3	Mid
		5th			
	2	6th		2	
		4th			
Low	1			1	Low

First Tone (High Level: 55)	sī	'silk'	represented by the level tone mark
Second Tone (High Rising: 35)	sí	'history'	represented by the rising tone mark
Third Tone (Mid Level: 33)	si	'try'	indicated by the absence of a tone mark
Fourth Tone (Low Falling: 21)	sìh	'time'	represented by the falling tone mark and 'h' indicating low level pitch
Fifth Tone (Low Rising: 23)	síh	'city'	represented by the rising tone mark and 'h' indicating low level pitch
Sixth Tone (Low Level: 22)	sih	'matter'	represented by the absence of a tone mark except 'h' which indicates low level pitch

Conventions used in this phrase book

1. Syllables are joined together to form words. The joining of syllables is called juncture and this process helps you to look at sounds as an integral unit rather than disjoined syllables. Where juncture creates confusion as to where one syllable ends and the next syllable begins, an apostrophe is used to indicate that juncture exists, e.g. wìhng'yúhn 'forever'.

2. For a syllable containing a diphthong or a triphthong, the tone mark always falls on the first written vowel, e.g. kéuih 'he/she', háau 'test', covering the tone value of the whole syllable. In the syllables m̀h 'not' and ńgh 'five' which have no vowel letters, the tone mark is written over the consonants m̀ and ǵ respectively.

3. An asterisk written next to a syllable indicates a changed tone, e.g. Gwóngdūng-wá* 'Cantonese', Yīngmán* 'English' etc.

4. The hyphen is used to indicate:
   (a) numbers above ten, e.g. sahp-yih 'twelve', gáu-sahp-gáu 'ninety-nine'
   (b) verb-object constructions, e.g. cheung-gō 'sing'
   (c) verb with special markers, e.g. làih-jó 'came', làih-gán 'coming'
   (d) compound nouns modified by adjectives, e.g. Méihgwok-yàhn 'American/s';
   (e) comparative adjectives, e.g. chìh-dī 'later'
   (f) days of the week, months, e.g. Sīngkèih-yaht 'Sunday', Sahp-yuht 'October'
   (g) reduplicated forms of nouns and adjectives, e.g. chī-lahp-lahp 'sticky'
   (h) adverbs ending in -ly, e.g. póupin-gám* 'generally'

Useful lists

1.1 Today or tomorrow? 10

1.2 Legal holidays 11

1.3 What time is it? 12

1.4 One, two, three... 14

1.5 The weather 17

1.6 Here, there... 18

1.7 What does that sign say? 19

1.8 Personal details 20

1 Useful lists

1.1 Today or tomorrow?

What day is it today?	今日係星期 / 禮拜幾? Gāmyaht haih sīngkèih/láihbaai-géi?
Today's Monday	今日係星期一 / 禮拜一 Gāmyaht haih sīngkèih/láihbaai-yāt.
Tuesday	星期 / 禮拜二 Sīngkèih/láihbaai-yih
Wednesday	星期 / 禮拜三 Sīngkèih/láihbaai-sāam
Thursday	星期 / 禮拜四 Sīngkèih/láihbaai-sei
Friday	星期 / 禮拜五 Sīngkèih/láihbaai-ńgh
Saturday	星期 / 禮拜六 Sīngkèih/láihbaai-luhk
Sunday	星期 / 禮拜日 Sīngkèih/láihbaai-yaht
in January	(喺 / 響) 一月 (hái/héung) Yātyuht
since February	二月到而家 Yihyuht dou yìhgā.
in spring	(喺 / 響) 春天 (hái/héung) chēuntīn
in summer	(喺 / 響) 夏天 (hái/héung) hahtīn
in autumn	(喺 / 響) 秋天 (hái/héung) chāuntīn
in winter	(喺 / 響) 冬天 (hái/héung) dūngtīn
2003	二零零三年 Yihlìnglìhngsāam-nìhn
the twentieth century	二十世紀 Yih-sahp-saigéi
the twenty-first century	二十一世紀 Yih-sahp-yāt-saigéi
What's the date today?	今日係幾號? Gāmyaht haih géi houh?
Today's the 24th	今日係二十四號。 Gāmyaht haih yih-sahp-sei-houh.
Wednesday, 3 November	十一月三號, 星期 / 禮拜三 Sahp-yāt-yuht sāam-houh, Sīngkèih/láihbaai-sāam
in the morning	(喺 / 響) 朝早 / 朝頭早 (hái/héung) jīujóu/jīutàuhjóu
in the afternoon	(喺 / 響) 下晝 (hái/héung) hahjau

in the evening	（喺／響）夜晚 (hái/héung) yehmáahn
at night	（喺／響）夜晚黑 (hái/héung) yehmáahn(hāk)
this morning	今朝早 gām jīujóu
this afternoon	今日下晝 gāmyaht hahjau
this evening	今晚 gāmmáahn
tonight	今晚（黑） gāmmáahn(hāk)
last night	琴／尋晚（黑） kàhm/chàhm'máahn(hāk)
tomorrow night	聽晚（黑） tīngmáahn(hāk)
this week	呢個星期／禮拜 nī go sīngkèih
last week	上個星期／禮拜 seuhng go sīngkèih/láihbaai
next week	下個星期／禮拜 hah go sīngkèih/láihhai
this month	呢個月 nī go yuht
last month	上個月 seuhng go yuht
next month	下個月 hah go yuht
this year	今年 gām'nín*/nìhn
last year	舊年 gauh'nín*/nìhn
next year	明／出年 mìhng/chēut'nín*/nìhn
in...days/weeks/ months/years	…日／星期／月／年之後 yaht/ sīngkèih/ yuht/ nìhn jīhauh
...weeks ago	…（個）星期／禮拜之前 …(go) sīngkèih/ láihbaai jīchìhn
two weeks ago	兩個星期／禮拜之前 léugng go sīngkèih/láihbaai jīchìhn
day off	放假 fongga

 **.2 Legal holidays**

● **In Hong Kong,** people celebrate both the Western New Year and Chinese New Year, the former with one day and the latter three days off from work. Western holidays such as Christmas and Easter are also observed with two off days for each to celebrate the festivities. Two special days off to show respects for ancestors: the Chingming

Festival is now celebrated on April 5, and the Chungyeung Festival on October 4 are such occasions. There is the Buddha's Birthday to balance the influence of Christmas and Easter and the occasion is celebrated on May 8. Traditional Chinese festivals follow the Lunar Calendar which identifies the months sequentially as the First Month, the Second Month, etc... Chinese New Year varies every year but falls between the last 10 days of January and the second 10 days of February of each year. The Dragon Boat Festival falls on the Fifth Day of the Fifth Lunar Month around the beginning of June and the Mid-Autumn Festival on the fifteenth day of the eighth month or mid-September. Since 1997, National Day and Labour Day are celebrated with a day off each. On these occasions, government institutions and banks are closed for business. Shopping centers and supermarkets keep normal opening hours from 11:00 a.m. till 9:00 p.m. Local shops vary, normally late into the night, and the convenience chain stores such as 7 Eleven and Circle K open 24 hours all days of the year.

January 1   *New Year's Day*
Sāilihk-sānnìhn / Yùhndaan   西曆新年 / 元旦

January/ February   *Chinese New Year* (Lunar Calendar:
First Day of the First Month)
Nùhnglihk-sānnìhn   農曆新年

March-April   *Easter*
[Sāam-yuht dou Sei-yuht jīgāan] Fuhkwuht-jit

April   *Festival of Sweeping Ancestors' Graves* (Lunar Calendar:
Third Day of the Third Month)
[Sei-yuht Ńgh-houh] Chīngmìhng-jit   清明節

May 1   *Labor Day*
[Ńgh-yuht Yāt-houh] Lòuhduhng-jit   勞動節

May 8   *The Buddha's Birthday*
[Ńgh-yuht Baat-houh] Wuhtfaht-jit   活佛節

June   *Dragon Boat Festival*
(Lunar Calendar: Fifth Day of the Fifth Month)
[Nùhnglihk Ńgh-yuht Ńgh-yaht] Dyūnńgh-jit   端午節

July 1   Hong Kong Special Administrative Region
Establishment Day
[Chāt-yuht Yāt-houh] Hēunggóng Dahkkēui sìhnglaahp-yaht 香港特區成立日

Mid-Autumn   *Mid-Autumn Festival*
[Nùhnglihk Baat-yuht Sahp-ńgh] Jūngchāu-jit   中秋節

October 1   *National Day*
[Sahp-yuht Yāt-houh] Gwokhing-jit   國慶節

October 4   *Chungyeung Festival*
[Sahp-yuht Sei-houh] Chùhngyèuhng-jit   重陽節

December 25   *Christmas Day*
[Sahp-yih-yuht Yih-sahp-ńgh-houh] Singdaan-jit   聖誕節

.3 What time is it?

What time is it?	而家幾點呀?
	Yìhgā géi dím a?
It's nine o'clock	而家九點。
	Yìhgā gáu dím.

five past ten	十點零五分／十點（踏）一／十點一個字 sahp dím lìhng ńgh fān / sahp dím (daahp) yāt / sahp dím yāt go jih
a quarter past eleven	十一點十五分／十一點（踏）三／ 十一點一個骨 sahp-yāt dím sahp-ńgh fān / sahp-yāt dím (daahp) sāam / sahp-yāt dím yāt go gwāt
twenty past twelve	十二點（踏）四／十二點四個字 sahp-yih dím (daahp) sei / sahp-yih dím sei go jih
half past one	一點半／一點三十分 yāt dím bun / yāt dím sāam-sahp fān
twenty-five to three	兩點（踏）七／兩點七個字 léuhng dím (daahp) chāt / léuhng dím chāt go jih
a quarter to four	三點（踏）九／三點三個骨／差一個骨四點 sāam dím (daahp) gáu / sāam dím sāam go gwāt / chā yāt go gwāt sei dím
ten to five	四點（踏）十／差兩個字五點 sei dím (daahp) sahp / chā léuhng go jih ńgh dím
It's midday (12:00 noon)	而家係中午十二點。 Yìhgā haih jūng'ńgh sahp-yih dím.
It's midnight	而家係晚黑十二點。 Yìhgā haih máahnhāk sahp-yih dím
half an hour	半個鐘頭 bun go jūngtàuh
What time?	幾點喇／而家幾點喇？ Géi dím la? / Yìhgā géi dím la?
What time can I come by?	我幾點可以過嚟呀？ Ngóh géi dím hóyíh gwo-làih a?
At...	喺...／響... hái/héung
After...	...之後 ... jìhauh
Before...	...之前 ... jìchìhn
Between 4:00 and 5:00	四點到五點之間 sei dím dou ńgh dím jìgāan
From...to...	從...到 chùhng....dou
In...minutes	...分鐘以後 ... fānjūng jìhauh
an hour	一個鐘頭之後 yāt go jūngtàuh jìhauh
two hours	兩個鐘頭之後 léuhng go jūngtàuh jìhauh
a quarter of an hour	一個骨鐘／十五分鐘／三個字 yāt go gwāt jūng / sahp-ńgh fānjūng / sāam go jih
three quarters of an hour	三個骨鐘／四十五分鐘／九個字 sāam go gwāt jūng / sei-sahp-ńgh fānjūng / gáu go jih
too early/late	太早／晏 taai jóu / ngaan/aan

on time _____ 準時
jéunsìh

summertime _____ 夏令時
(daylight saving) hahlihngsìh

wintertime _____ 冬季時間
dūnggwai sìhgaan

1.4 One, two, three...

0 _____ 零
lìhng

1 _____ 一
yāt

2 _____ 二
yih

3 _____ 三
sāam

4 _____ 四
sei

5 _____ 五
ńgh

6 _____ 六
luhk

7 _____ 七
chāt

8 _____ 八
baat

9 _____ 九
gáu

10 _____ 十
sahp

11 _____ 十一
sahp-yāt

12 _____ 十二
sahp-yih

13 _____ 十三
sahp-sāam

14 _____ 十四
sahp-sei

15 _____ 十五
sahp-ńgh

16 _____ 十六
sahp-luhk

17 _____ 十七
sahp-chāt

18 _____ 十八
sahp-baat

19 _____ 十九
sahp-gáu

20 _____ 二十
yih-sahp

21	二十一
	yih-sahp-yāt
22	二十二
	yih-sahp-yih
30	三十
	sāam-sahp
31	三十一
	sāam-sahp-yāt
32	三十二
	sāam-sahp-yih
40	四十
	sei-sahp
50	五十
	ńgh-sahp
60	六十
	luhk-sahp
70	七十
	chat-sahp
80	八十
	baat-sahp
90	九十
	gáu-sahp
100	一百
	yāt-baak
101	一百零一
	yāt-baak-lìhng-yāt
110	一百一十
	yāt-baak yāt-sahp
111	一百一十一
	yāt-baak-yāt-sahp-yāt
120	一百二十
	yāt-baak yih-sahp
200	二百 / 兩百
	yih-baak / léuhng-baak
300	三百
	sāam-baak
400	四百
	sei-baak
500	五百
	ńgh-baak
600	六百
	luhk-baak
700	七百
	chāt-baak
800	八百
	baat-baak
900	九百
	gáu-baak
1,000	一千
	yāt-chīn

1,100	一千一百	yāt-chīn-yāt-baak
2,000	二千 / 兩千	yih-chīn / léuhng-chīn
10,000	一萬	yāt-maahn
100,000	十萬	sahp-maahn
1,000,000	(一) 百萬	(yāt) baak-maahn
10,000,000	(一) 千萬	(yāt) chīn-maahn
1st	第一	daih-yāt
2nd	第二	daih-yih
3rd	第三	daih-sāam
4th	第四	daih-sei
once	一次	yāt chi
twice	兩次	léuhng chi
double	兩倍	léuhng-púih
triple	三倍	sāam-púih
half	一半	yātbun
a quarter	四分之一	seifahnjī-yāt
a third	三分之一	sāamfahnjī-yāt
some/a few	一啲 / 幾個	yātdī / géi go
$2 + 4 = 6$	二加四等如六	yih gā sei dángyùh luhk
$4 - 2 = 2$	四減二等如二	sei gáam yih dángyùh yih
$2 \times 4 = 8$	二乘四等如八	yih sìhng sei dángyùh baat
$4 \div 2 = 2$	四除二等如二	sei chèuih yih dángyùh yih
even/odd	雙數 / 單數	sēungsou/dāansou
total	一共	yātguhng
6×9	六乘九	luhk sìhng gáu

.5 The weather

Is the weather going to be good/bad?	天氣會好嗎? Tīnhei wúih hóu ma?
Is it going to get colder/hotter?	天氣會唔會凍 / 熱呀? Tīnhei wúih-m̀h-wúih dung / yiht a?
What temperature is it going to be?	今日氣溫幾多度呀? Gāmyaht heiwān géidō douh a?
Is it going to rain?	會唔會落雨呀? Wúih-m̀h-wúih lohk-yúh a?
Is there going to be a storm?	會唔會打風呀? Wúih-m̀h-wúih dá-fūng a?
Is it going to snow?	會唔會落雪呀? Wúih-m̀h-wúih lohk-syut a?
Is it going to freeze?	會唔會凍到結冰呀? Wúih-m̀h-wúih duhng-dou git-bīng a?
Is it going to be foggy?	會唔會大霧呀? Wúih-m̀h-wúih daaihmouh a?
Is there going to be a thunderstorm?	會唔會有雷陣雨呀? Wúih-m̀h-wúih yáuh lèuih-jahnyúh a?
The weather's changing.	天氣變喇。 Tīnhei bin la.
It's going to be cold.	天氣會凍。 Tīnhei wúih dung.
What's the weather going to be like today/tomorrow?	今日 / 聽日天氣會點呀? Gāmyaht/tīngyaht tīnhei wúih dím a?

悶熱。 sweltering/muggy	藍天 / 密雲 / 陰天 clear skies/cloudy/ overcast	又凍又潮濕 cold and damp
落霜 frost	好熱 very hot	霧 / 大霧 fog/foggy
落雨 rain	(攝氏) 度 ...degrees (Celsius)	潮濕 humid
晴朗 sunny	零下…度 ...degrees (below zero)	涼爽 cool
夜間落霜 overnight frost	晴朗 fine/clear	落雪 snow
翻風 gusts of wind	落大雨 heavy rain	颶風 hurricane
好天 fine	落冰雹 hail	又陰又凍 bleak
冰凍 / 冰冷 ice/icy	令人發悶嘅 stifling	多雲狀態 cloudiness
暴雨 / 傾盆大雨 downpour	微風 / 疾風 / 狂風 moderate/strong/very strong winds	風 wind
霜 / 寒冷 frost/frosty	和暖 mild	熱風 heatwave
晴 / 天晴 sunny day	暴風雨 storm	大風 windy

Useful lists

.6 Here, there...

See also 5.1 Asking for directions

here, over here / there, over there	呢度 / 嗰度 nīdouh/gódouh
somewhere	某個地方 máuh go deihfōng
everywhere	到處 dou'chyu
far away/nearby	好遠 / 附近 hóu yúhn / fuhgahn
(on the) right/ (on the) left	(喺 / 響) 右 / 左邊 hái/héung yauh/jó'bihn
to the right/left of	靠右 / 左邊 kaau yauh / jó'bihn
straight ahead	一直向前走 yātjihk heung chìhn jáu
via	經過 gīnggwo
in	(喺 / 響) … 入邊 / 面 (hái/héung) ... yahp'bihn/mihn
on	(喺 / 響) … 上邊 / 面 (hái/héung) ... seuhng'bihn/mihn
under	(喺 / 響) … 下邊 / 面 (hái/héung) ... hah'bihn/mihn
against	挨住 ngāaijyuh
opposite/facing	對面 / 對住 deui'mihn/deuijyuh
next to	喺 / 響 … 旁邊 hái/héung ... pòhngbīn
near	近住 gahnjyuh
in front of	喺 / 響 … 前面 hái/héung ... chìhnmihn
in the center	喺 / 響 … 中間 hái/héung ... jūnggāan
forward	向前 heungchìhn
down	向下 heunghah
up	向上 heungseuhng
inside	入邊 / 面 yahp'bihn/mihn
outside	外邊 / 面 ngoih'bihn/mihn
behind	後邊 / 面 hauh'bihn/mihn

at the front of _____	喺 / 響 … 前面
	hái/héung … chìhnmihn
at the back of _____	喺 / 響 … 後面
	hái/héung … hauhmihn
in the north of _____	喺 / 響 … 北邊
	hái/héung … bākbihn
to the south of _____	喺 / 響 … 以南
	hái/héung … yíh nàahm
from the west _____	喺 / 響西邊嚟
	hái/héung sāibihn làih
from the east _____	喺 / 響東邊嚟
	hái/héung dūngbihn làih

.7 What does that sign say?

路牌 traffic signs	出售 for sale	警察局 police
出租 for hire	郵局 post office	醫院 hospital
賣完 sold out	高壓電 high voltage	消防局 fire department
候機室 / 候車室 waiting room	詢問處 information	兌換 exchange
熱水 / 凍水 hot/cold water	(緊急) 出口 (emergency) exit	行人 pedestrians
緊急煞掣 emergency brake	打開 open	售款處 cashier
安全出口 / 消防通道 fire escape	(免費) 入場 entrance (free)	危險 / 易燃物品 / 致命 danger/fire hazard/danger to life
非飲用水 water (not for drinking)	提防惡狗 beware of the dog	
	請勿騷擾 / 觸摸 please do not disturb/touch	休假 / 裝修期內 / 停止營業 closed (for holiday/ refurbishment)
停用 not in use	油漆未乾 wet paint	
推 push	危險 danger	交通警察 traffic police
出租 for rent	冇人 vacant	客滿 / 滿座 full
洗手間 bathrooms	有人 engaged	急救室 / 急癥室 first aid/accident and emergency (hospital)
拉 pull	請勿吸烟 no smoking/no litter	
酒店 / 旅館 hotel	請勿隨地拋弃垃圾 no litter	
待維修 out of order	售票處 ticket office	禁止打獵 / 釣魚 no hunting/fishing
旅遊咨詢處 tourist information bureau	時間表 timetable	預定席 reserved
停 (止) stop	此路不通 / 禁止入內 no access/no entry	入口 entrance

1.8 Personal details

● **In Chinese societies,** the family name comes first and the given name next. Titles come after the name. For example, Mr Wong is Wòhng sīnsāang 黃先生 and Ms Wong is either Wòhng síujé 黃小姐 or Wòhng néuihsih 黃女士 (for women in their late 50s and above). The title taaitáai* 太太 is given to married women and is placed after the husband's surname. This is the convention still used by Chinese women in Hong Kong, Macau, Taiwan and outside China. In Mainland China, however, Chinese women now do not adopt their husband's surname after marriage.

surname	姓 sing
first name	名 méng*
address (street/number)	地址（街名／門牌號碼） deihjí (gāaiméng* / mùhnpàaih houhmáh)
postal code/town	郵編號碼／城市 yàuhpīn houhmáh / sìhngsíh
sex (male/female)	性別（男／女） singbiht (nàahm/néuih)
nationality/citizenship	國籍 gwokjihk
date of birth	出生日期 chēutsāng yahtkèih
place of birth	出生地點 chēutsāng deihdím
occupation	職業 jīkyihp
marital status	婚烟狀況 fānyān johngtaai
married/single	已婚／未婚 yíhfāan / meihfān
widowed	寡婦／鰥夫 gwáfúh / gwāanfū
(number of) children	兒女（數目） yìhnéuih (soumuhk)
passport/identity card/ driving license number	護照／身份證／駕駛執照號碼 wuhjiu / sānfán*-jing / gasái-jāpjiu houhmáh
place and date of issue	簽發地點／簽發日期 chīmfaat deihdím/chīmfaat yahtkèih
signature	簽名 chīmméng*

Courtesies

2.1 Greetings   22

2.2 How to ask a question   23

2.3 How to reply   25

2.4 Thank you   25

2.5 Sorry   26

2.6 What do you think?   26

2 Courtesies

● **It is usual** in Hong Kong to shake hands on meeting and parting company. The strength of the handshakes is determined by the level of acquaintance and the importance of the occasion. Generally one should refrain from giving a strong handshake to male or female acquaintances. Hugging is reserved for relatives and kissing on the cheeks is now more common among Cantonese speaking Chinese communities in different parts of the world.

2.1 Greetings

Good morning, Mr Williams	早晨，威廉先生！ Jóusàhng, Wāiìihm sīnsāang!
Hello/Good morning, Mrs Jones	早晨，鐘士太太*！ Jóusàhng, Jūngsih taaitáai*!
Hello, Peter	你好，彼德！ Néih hóu, Pītàh!
Hi, Helen	你好，海倫！ Néih hóu, Hēlàhn!
Good morning, madam	早晨，太太／夫人 Jóusàhn, taaitáai/fūyàhn!
Good afternoon, sir	您好！ Néih hóu!
Good afternoon/evening	你好！ Néih hóu!
How are you?	你好嗎？ Néih hóu ma?
Fine, thank you, and you?	幾好，有心，你呢？ Géi hóu, yáuh sām, néih nē?
Very well, and you?	幾好，你呢？ Géi hóu, néih nē?
In excellent health/In great shape	精神好／身體好 Jīngsàhn hóu / Sāntái hóu.
So-so	過得去啦／麻麻哋啦。 Gwo-dāk heui lā / Màhmá*déi* lā.
Not very well	唔係咁好。 M̀h'haih gam hóu.
Not bad	唔錯／算係噉啦。 M̀h'cho / Syun haih gám* lā.
I'm going to leave	我走先。 Ngóh jáu sīn.
I have to be going, someone's waiting for me	我要走喇，有人等緊我。 Ngóh yiu jáu la, yáuh yàhn dáng-gán ngóh.
Good-bye	拜拜！ Bāaibaai!
See you later	再見！ Joigin!
See you soon	第日見！ Daihyaht gin!

See you in a little while!	一陣間見!
	Yātjahn'gāan gin!

Sweet dreams!	發個甜夢!
	Faat go tìhm muhng!

Good night!	早抖!
	Jóutáu!

All the best/Good luck!	祝你好運!
	Jūk néih hóu wahn!

Have fun!	玩開心啲!
	Wáan hōisām-dī!

Have a nice vacation!	假期愉快!
	Gakèih yuhfaai!

Bon voyage/ Have a good trip	一路順風! / 旅途愉快!
	Yāt-louh seuhnfūng! / léuihtòuh yuhfaai!

Thank you, the same to you	多謝你, 你都係噉話。
	Dōjeh néih, néih dōu haih gám wah.

Say hello to/Give my regards to... (formal)	請代我問候…
	Chíng doih ngóh mahnhauh ...

Say hello to... (informal)	幫我問候…
	Bōng ngóh mahnhauh ...

2.2 How to ask a question

Who's that?/Who is it?	邊個 / 邊位?
	Bīn go? / Bīn wái*?

What?	乜嘢?
	Mātyéh?

What is there to see?	有乜嘢睇呀?
	Yáuh mātyéh tái a?

What category of hotel is it?	呢間酒店係幾星級㗎?
	Nī gāan jáudim haih géi sīngkāp ga?

Where?	邊度? / 邊處?
	bīndouh/bīnsyu?

Where's the bathroom?	洗手間喺 / 響邊度呀?
	Sáisáu-gāan hái/héung bīndouh a?

Where are you going?	你去邊度 / 邊處呀?
	Néih heui bīndouh/bīnsyu a?

Where are you from?	你喺邊度嚟㗎?
	Néih hái bīndouh làih ga?

What?/How?	乜嘢 / 點樣?
	Mātyéh? / Dímyéung*?

What's your name? (formal)	貴姓呀? / 應該點稱呼你呀?
	Gwai sing a? / Yīnggōi dím chīngfū néih a?

What's your name? (informal)	你叫做乜嘢名呀?
	Néih giujouh mātyé méng* a?

How far is that?	有幾遠呀?
	Yáuh géi yúhn a?

How long does that take?	要幾耐呀? / 要幾長時間呀?
	Yiu géi noih a / Yiu géi chèuhng sìhgaan a?

How long is the trip?	呢次旅行去幾耐呀? / 去幾長時間呀?
	Nī chi léuihhàhng heui géi noih a / heui géi chèuhng sìhgaan a?

How much?	幾多錢?
	Géidō chín*?
How much is this?	呢個幾多錢?
	Nī go géidō chín*?
What time is it?	而家幾點喇?
	Yìhgā géidím la?
Which one/s?	邊個 / 邊啲?
	Bīn go / Bīn dī?
Which glass is mine?	邊個杯係我㗎?
	Bīn go būi haih ngóh ga?
When?	幾時?
	Géisìh?
When are you leaving? (formal)	你幾時 / 幾點出發?
	Néih géisìh/géidím chēutfaat?
Why?	點解?
	Dímgáai?
Could you...? (formal)	可唔可以…? / 唔該…
	Hó-m̀h-hóyíh ... ? / m̀h'gōi ...
Could you help me/ give me a hand please?	可唔可以幫我…? / 唔該幫我…
	Hó-m̀h-hóyíh bōng ngóh... ? / m̀h'gōi bōng ngóh...
Could you point that out to me/show me please?	唔該指 / 攞俾我睇吓?
	M̀h'gōi jí/ló béi ngóh tái-háh.
Could you come with me, please?	唔該跟我嚟。
	M̀h'gōi gān ngóh làih.
Could you reserve/book me some tickets please?	唔該幫我預訂幾張飛。
	M̀h'gōi bōng ngóh yuhdehng géi jēung fēi.
Could you recommend another hotel?	唔該你推薦第二間酒店俾我。
	M̀h'gōi néih tēuijin daihyih gāan jáudim béi ngóh.
Do you know...? (formal)	你知唔知…?
	Néih jī-m̀h-jī ... ?
Do you know whether...?	係唔係…?
	Haih-m̀h-haih ... ?
Do you have...?	你(哋)有冇…?
	Néih(deih) yáuh-móuh ... ?
Do you have a vegetarian dish, please?	呢度有冇齋食呀?
	Nīdouh yáuh-móuh jāai sihk a?
I would like...	我想要（一个）?
	Ngóh séung yiu (yāt go) ...
I'd like a kilo of apples, please	唔該俾我一公斤蘋果。
	M̀h'gōi béi ngóh yāt gūnggān pìhnggwó.
Can/May I?	我可以…嗎?
	Ngóh hóyíh ... ma?
Can/May I take this away?	我可以拎走嗎?
	Ngóh hóyíh līng-jáu ma?
Can I smoke here?	我可以喺 / 響呢度食煙嗎?
	Ngóh hóyíh hái/héung nīdouh sihk-yīn ma?
Could I ask you something?	我可以問你啲嘢嗎?
	Ngóh hóyíh mahn néih dī yéh ma?

2.3 How to reply

My name is ... — 我姓 / 我叫做…
Ngóh sing ... / Ngóh giujouh ....

Yes, of course — 係，當然啦。
Haih, dōngyihn lā.

No, I'm sorry — 唔係，對唔住！
Mh'haih, deui'mh-jyuh!

Yes, what can I do for you? — 我就係，有啲乜嘢我可以幫到你呢？
Ngóh jauh haih. Yáuh dī mātyéh ngóh hóyíh bōng-dóu néih nē?

Just a moment, please — 唔該等一陣。
Mh'gōi dáng yātjahn.

No, I don't have time now — 對唔住！我而家唔得閒。
Deui'mh-jyuh, ngóh yìhga mh'dākhàahn!

No, that's impossible — 對唔住！我做唔到。
Deui'mh-jyuh, ngóh jouh-mh-dóu*.

I think so/I think that's absolutely right — 我諗係嘅 / 你講得好啱。
Ngóh nám haih gám./ Néih góng-dāk hóu ngāam!

I think so too/I agree — 我都係嘅諗 / 我同意。
Ngóh dōu haih gám nám./ Ngóh tùhngyi!

I hope so too — 我都希望係嘅。
Ngóh dōu hēimohng haih gám.

No, not at all/ Absolutely not — 唔係，唔係嘅樣。 / 絕對唔係。
Mh'haih, mh'haih gámyéung*. / Jyuhtdeui mh'haih.

No, no one — 冇，冇人。
Móuh, móuhyàhn.

No, nothing — 冇，乜嘢都冇。
Móuh, mātyéh dōu móuh.

That's right — 冇錯
Móuhcho.

Something's wrong — 有啲唔妥 / 有啲問題
Yáuh dī mh'tóh/yáuh dī mahntàih.

I agree (don't agree) — 我同意 / 唔同意
Ngóh tùhngyi/mh'tùhngyi.

OK/It's fine — 得嘞，冇問題。
Dāk laak, móuh mahntàih.

OK, all right — 得嘞，搞掂。
Dāk laak, gáaudihm.

Perhaps/maybe — 或者係 / 有可能
Waahkjé haih / yáuh hó'nàhng.

I don't know — 我唔知(道)。
Ngóh mh'jī(dou).

2.4 Thank you

Thank you — 唔該 / 多謝！
Mh'gōi/dōjeh!

You're welcome — 唔駛客氣。
Mh'sái haakhei.

Thank you very much/	唔該晒／多謝晒。
Many thanks	M̀h'gōi-saai / dōjeh-saai
Very kind of you _____	你太客氣喇。
	Néih taai haakhei la.
My pleasure _____	應該嘅。
	Yīnggōi gé*
I enjoyed it very much _____	好好食，我食咗好多。
(food)	Hóuhóu sihk, ngóh sihk-jó hóudō.
I enjoyed it very _____	玩得好開心。
much (game, tour etc)	Wáan*-dāk hóu hōisām.
Thank you for _____	多謝你俾我嘅…
	Dōjeh néih béi ngóh ge ...
You shouldn't have/ _____	你真係太客氣嘞。
That was so kind of you	Néih jānhaih taai haakhei laak.
Don't mention it! _____	不／唔成敬意。
	Bāt/M̀h'sìhng-gingyi!
That's all right _____	少少意思啫。
	Síusíu yisi jē.

2.5 Sorry

Excuse me/Pardon me/ _____	請問／唔好意思／對唔住。
Sorry (formal)	Chíngmahn / m̀h'hóu yisi / deui'm̀h-jyuh
Sorry, I didn't know that... _____	對唔住，我唔知道…
	Deui'm̀h-jyuh, ngóh m̀h'jīdou ...
Excuse/Pardon me _____	請問／唔好意思。
(formal)	chíngmahn / m̀h'hóu yisi
I do apologize _____	我真誠道歉。／真係對唔住嘞。
(formal/informal)	Ngóh jānsìhng douhhip. / Jānhaih deui'm̀h-jyuh laak.
I'm sorry _____	對唔住
	Deui'm̀h-jyuh.
I didn't mean it/ _____	我唔係故意㗎。／呢個係意外。
It was an accident	Ngóh m̀h'haih guyi ga. / Nī go haih yi'ngoih.
That's all right/Don't _____	唔緊要／冇所謂。
worry about it (formal)	M̀h'gányiu/ Móuhsówaih
Never mind/Forget it _____	冇事／算啦。
(informal)	Móuhsih/Syun lā.
It could happen to anyone _____	呢件事可能發生喺／響任何人身上。
	Nī gihn sih hó'nàhng faatsāng hái/héung yahmhòh-yàhn sānseuhng.

2.6 What do you think?

Which do you prefer?/ _____	你最鐘意邊(個)？
like best? (formal)	Néih jeui jūngyi bīn(go)?
What do you think? _____	你覺得點呀？
(informal)	Néih gokdāk dím a?
Don't you like dancing? _____	你唔鐘意跳舞咩？
	Néih m̀h'jūngyi tiumóuh mē?

I don't mind _____	我唔介意。 Ngóh m̀h'gaaiyi.
Well done! _____	做得太好了! Jouh-dāk taai hóu laak!
Not bad! _____	唔錯吖! M̀h'cho ā!
Great!/Marvellous! _____	好極嘞! Hóugihk laak!
Wonderful! _____	太好嘞! Taai hóu laak!
How lovely! _____	太靚嘞! Taai leng laak!
I am pleased for you. _____	我嗲你開心。 Ngóh dahng néih hōisām.
I'm very happy/ _____ delighted to...	我好開心 / 高興… Ngóh hóu hōisām/gōuhing ...
It's really nice here! _____	呢度周圍都好靚! Nīdouh jauwàih dō hóu leng!
How nice! _____	真好! Jān hóu!
I'm very happy with... _____	我對…好滿意。 Ngóh deui ... hóu múhnyi.
I'm (not) very happy with... _____	我對…唔滿意。 Ngóh deui ... m̀h'múhnyi.
I'm glad that.... _____	我好開心… Ngóh hóu hōisām ...
I'm having a great time. _____	我玩得好開心。 Ngóh wáan dāk hóu hōisām.
I can't wait till tomorrow _____	我真係想聽日快啲嚟。 Ngóh jūnhaih séung tīngyaht faai-dī làih.
I'm looking forward to _____ tomorrow	我期望聽日嘅來臨。 Ngóh kèihmohng tīngyaht ge lòihlàhm.
I hope it works out _____	希望一切進行順利。 Hēimohng yātchai jeunhàhng seuhnleih.
How awful! _____	太差勁喇! Taai chāgihng la!
It's horrible _____	太恐怖喇! Taai húngbou la!
That's ridiculous! _____	太可笑喇! Taai hósiu la!
That's terrible! _____	太可怕喇! Taai hópa la!
What a pity/shame! _____	真係可惜! Jānhaih hósīk!
How disgusting! _____	真係令人反胃! Jānhaih lihng yàhn fáanwaih!
What nonsense/ _____ How silly!	真係廢話! / 真係胡鬧! Jānhaih faiwá*/ Jānhaih wùh'naauh!
I don't like it/them _____	我唔鐘意嗰个 / 啲。 Ngóh m̀h'jūngyi gó go/dī.

Conversation

3.1 **I** beg your pardon? 29

3.2 **I**ntroductions 29

3.3 **S**tarting/ending a
conversation 32

3.4 **C**ongratulations and
condolences 32

3.5 **A** chat about the
weather 33

3.6 **H**obbies 33

3.7 **B**eing the host(ess) 33

3.8 **I**nvitations 34

3.9 **P**aying a compliment 35

3.10 **I**ntimate comments/
questions 35

3.11 **A**rrangements 36

3.12 **S**aying good-bye 37

3 Conversation

3.1 I beg your pardon?

I don't speak any/ I speak a little...	我唔識講… / 我識講少少… Ngóh m̀h'sīk góng ... / Ngóh sīk góng síusíu ...
I'm American	我係美國人。 Ngóh haih Méihgwok-yàhn.
Do you speak English? (formal)	你識唔識講英文呀？ Néih sīk-m̀h-sīk góng Yīngmán* a?
Is there anyone who speaks...?	呢度有冇人認識講…？ Nīdouh yáuh-móuh yàhn sīk góng ... ?
I beg your pardon/What?	咩話？ Mē'wá*?
I (don't) understand	我聽唔明。 Ngóh tēng m̀h'mìhng.
Do you understand me? (formal)	你明唔明我講乜嘢呀？ Néih mìhng-m̀h-mìhng ngóh góng mātyéh a?
Could you repeat that, please?	唔該(你)再講一次。 M̀h'gōi (néih) joi góng yāt chi.
Could you speak more slowly, please?	唔該(你)講慢啲。 M̀h'gōi (néih) góng maahn-dī.
What does this/ that mean?	點解呀？ Dímgáai a?
It's more or less the same as...	同…差唔多意思。 Tùhng ... chā'm̀h-dō yisī.
Could you write that down for me, please?	唔該幫我寫低。 M̀h'gōi bōng ngóh sé-dāi.
Could you spell that for me, please?	唔該用字母拼出嚟。 M̀h'gōi yuhng jihmóuh ping-chēut-làih.
Could you point to the phrase in this book, please?	唔該喺 / 響呢本書(呢)度指俾我睇。 M̀h'gōi hái/héung nī bún syū (nī)douh jí béi ngóh tái.
Just a minute, I'll look it up	唔該等一陣，我查一吓。 M̀h'gōi dáng yātjahn, ngóh chàh-yātháh,
I can't find the word/ the sentence	我搵唔到呢個詞 / 呢句話。 Ngóh wán'm̀h-dóu nī go chìh / nī geui wah.
How do you say that in...?	用…點講？ Yuhng ... dím góng?
How do you pronounce that word?	呢個字點讀？ Nī go jih dím duhk ?

3.2 Introductions

May I introduce myself?	等我自我介紹一吓 Dáng ngóh jih'ngóh gaaisiuh-yātháh.
My name's...	我叫做… Ngóh giujouh ...
I'm...	我係… Ngóh haih ...

Conversation

What's your name? (formal)	請問，貴姓呀？ Chíng'mahn, gwai sing a?
What's your name? (informal)	你叫做乜嘢名呀？ Néih giujouh mātyéh méng* a?
May I introduce...?	我嚟介紹，呢位係…，呢位係… Ngóh làih gaaisiuh, nī wái* haih..., nī wái* haih...
This is my wife/husband	呢位係我太太…我先生… Nī wái* haih ngoh taaitáai* ... / ngóh sīnsāang ...
This is my daughter/son	呢個係我個女 / 仔… Nī go haih ngóh go néui*/jái ...
This is my mother/ father	呢位係我媽媽 / 我爸爸。 Nī wái* haih ngóh màhmā / bàhbā .
This is my fiancée/fiancé	呢位係我未婚妻 / 未婚夫… Nī wái* haih ngóh meihfān-chāi/meihfān-fū ...
This is my girl/boy friend.	呢位係我女朋友 / 男朋友… Nī wái* haih ngóh néuihpàhngyáuh/ nàahmpàhngyáuh.
This is my friend	呢位係我朋友。… Nī wái* haih ngóh pàhngyáuh, ...
How do you do?	你好嗎？ Néih hóu ma?
Hi, pleased to meet you (informal).	你好！ Néih hóu!
Pleased to meet you (formal).	幸會！ / 好高興認識你。 Hahng'wuih! / Hóu gōuhing yihngsīk néih.
Where are you from? (formal/informal)	你喺 / 響邊嚟㗎？ Néih hái/héung bīndouh làih ga?
I'm American	我係美國人。 Ngóh haih Méihgwok-yàhn.
What city do you live in?	你住喺 / 響邊個城市？ Néih jyuh hái/héung bīn go sìhngsíh?
In.../near...	喺 / 響… / 靠近… Hái/héung... / Kaaugahn ...
Have you been here long?	你嚟咗呢度幾耐？ Néih làih-jó nīdouh géi noih?
A few days	幾日。 Géi yaht.
How long are you staying here?	你打算喺 / 響呢度住幾耐？ Néih dásyun hái/héung nīdouh jyuh géi noih?
We'll (probably) be leaving tomorrow.	我哋（或者）聽日走。 Ngóhdeih (waahkjé) tīngyaht jáu.
We'll (probably) be leaving in two weeks.	我哋（或者）兩個星期 / 禮拜後走。 Ngóhdeih (waahkjé) léuhng go sīngkèih/ láihbaai hauh jáu.
Where are you staying?	你住喺 / 響邊度？ Néih jyuh hái/héung bīndouh?
I'm staying in a hotel.	我住喺 / 響酒店。 Ngóh jyuh hái/héung jáudim.
I'm staying with friends/ relatives.	我住喺 / 響朋友 / 親戚屋企。 Ngóh jyuh háihéung pàhngyáuh/chānchīk ngūkkéi*.

3

Are you here on your own?/Are you here with your family?	你自己一個人嚟啊？／你同家人嚟啊？ Néih jihgéi yāt go yàhn làih àh? / Néih tùhng gāyàhn làih àh?
I'm on my own.	我自己一個人嚟。 Ngóh jihgéi yāt go yàhn làih.
I'm with my wife/husband	我同我太太／先生一齊嚟。 Ngóh tùhng ngóh taaitáai/sīnsāang yātchàih làih.
– with my family	同家人嚟。 tùhng gāyàhn làih
– with relatives	同親戚嚟 tùhng chānchīk làih
– with a friend/friends	同一個／幾個朋友嚟 tùhng yāt go / géi go pàngyáuh làih
Are you married?	你結咗婚未呀？ Néih git-jó-fān meih a?
Do you have a steady boy/girlfriend?	你有女朋友／男朋友未呀？ Néih yáuh néuihpàhngyáuh/ nàahmpàhngyáuh meih a?
I'm married.	我結咗婚。 Ngóh git-jó-fān.
I'm single.	我係單身嘅。 Ngóh haih dāansān ge.
I'm not married.	我仲未結婚。 Ngóh juhng meih gitfān.
I'm separated.	我分咗居。 Ngóh fān-jó-gēui.
I'm divorced.	我離咗婚。 Ngóh lèih-jó-fān.
I'm a widow/widower	我丈夫／老婆過咗身。 Ngóh jeuhngfū/lóuhpòh gwo-jó-sāng.
I live alone.	我自己一個人住。 Ngóh jihgéi yāt go yàhn jyuh.
Do you have any children/grandchildren?	你有冇細蚊仔／孫呀？ Néih yáuh-móuh saimānjái/syūn a?
How old are you?	你幾大喇？ Néih géi daaih la? (young people) 你幾大年紀喇？ Néih géi daaih nìhn'géi la? (older people)
How old is she/he?	佢／幾大年紀喇？ Kéuih géi daaih nìhn'géi la?
I'm...(years old)	我今年…歲。 Ngóh gāmnìhn ... seui.
She's/he is...(years old).	佢今年…歲。 Kéuih gāmnihn ... seui.
What do you do for a living?	你做乜嘢工作㗎？ Néih jouh mātyéh gūngjok ga?
I work in an office.	我喺寫字樓做事嘅。 Ngóh hái séjih-làuh jouhsih ge.
I'm a student.	我係學生 Ngóh haih hohksāang.

I'm unemployed.	我失咗業。 Ngóh sāt-jó-yihp.
I'm retired.	我退咗休。 Ngóh teui-jó-yāu.
I'm on a disability pension.	我而家領傷殘撫恤金。 Ngóh yìhgā líhng sēungchàahn fúsēut-gām.
I'm a housewife.	我係家庭主婦。 Ngóh haih gātìhng jyúfúh.
Do you like your job?	你鐘意你嘅工作嗎? Néih jūngyi néih ge gūngjok ma?
Most of the time.	大部份時間鐘意。 Daaih-bouhfahn sìhgaan jūngyi.
Mostly I do, but I prefer vacations.	雖然我唔意做工,不過都係放假好。 Sēuiyìhn ngóh m̀h'gaaiyi jouh-gūng, bātgwo dōu haih fong-ga hóu.

3.3 Starting/ending a conversation

Could I ask you something?	我可以問你的嘢嗎? Ngóh hóyíh mahn néih dī yéh ma?
Excuse/Pardon me (formal/informal)	請問... Chíngmahn...
Could you help me please?	你可唔可以幫我呀? Néih hó-m̀h-hóyíh bōng ngóh a?
Yes, what's the problem?	得,乜嘢事呀? Dāk, mātyéh sih a?
What can I do for you?	有乜嘢(我)可以幫到你㗎? Yáuh mātyéh (ngóh) hóyíh bōng-dóu néih ga?
Sorry, I don't have time now	唔好意思,我而家好忙。 M̀h'hóu yisi, ngóh yìhgā hóu mòhng.
Do you have a light?	唔該借個火. M̀h'gōi je go fó.
May I join you?	我可以加入(你哋)嗎? Ngóh hóyíh gā-yahp (néihdeih) ma?
Can I take a picture?	我可以影張相嗎? Ngóh hóyíh yíng jēung séung* ma?
Could you take a picture of me/us?	可以幫(我 / 我哋)影張相嗎? Hóyíh bōng ngóh yíng jēung séung* ma?
Leave me alone	唔好煩我。 M̀h'hóu fàahn ngóh.
Get lost (formal/informal)	行開 / 走開! Hàhng-hōi!/Jáu-hōi!
Go away or I'll scream	你再走開我嗌㗎喇。 Néih joi m̀h'jáu-hōi ngóh jauh ngaai ga la.

3.4 Congratulations and condolences

Happy birthday	(祝你)生日快樂! (Jūk néih) sāangyaht faailohk!
Many happy returns	(祝你)一切順利! (Jūk néih) yātchai seuhnleih!

Please accept my _____ 請接受我嘅慰問。
condolences   Chíng jipsauh ngóh ge waimahn.

My deepest sympathy ____ 請接受我最深切嘅同情。
                          Chíng jipsauh ngóh jeui sāmchit ge tùhngchìhng.

3.5 A chat about the weather

See also 1.5 The weather

It's so hot/cold today! ____ 今日好熱／凍！
                            Gāmyaht hóu yiht/dung!

Isn't it a lovely day? _____ 今日真係陽光普照！
                             Gāmyaht jān haih yèuhnggwōng póujiu!

It's so windy/What a storm! _ 好大風呀／風太大喇。
                             Hóu daaihfūng a / Fūng taai daaih la.

All that rain/snow! _____ 落咁大嘅雨／雪！
                            Lohk gam daaih ge yúh/syut!

It's so foggy! _____ 好大霧呀！
                           Hóu daaih mouh a!

Has the weather been ____ 嗰嘅天氣好耐囉？
like this for long?   Gám ge tīnhei hóu noih làh?

Is it always this hot/ _____ 呢度嘅天氣成日都咁熱／凍㗎？
cold here?   Nīdouh ge tīnhei sèhngyaht dōu gam yiht/
                           dung gàh?

Is it always this dry/ _____ 呢度嘅天氣成日都咁乾燥／潮濕㗎？
humid here?   Nīdouh ge tīnhei sèhngyaht dōu gam gōncho/
                           chìuhsāp gàh?

3.6 Hobbies

Do you have any _____ 你有乜嘢愛好？
hobbies?   Néih yáuh mātyéh ngoihou?

I like knitting/reading/ _____ 我鐘意織冷衫／睇書／影相。
photography.   Ngóh jūngyi jīk-lāangsāam/tái-syū/yíngséung*.

I enjoy listening to music. _ 我鐘意聽音樂。
                           Ngóh jūngyi tēng yām'ngohk.

I play the guitar/piano. ____ 我鐘意彈吉他／鋼琴。
                           Ngóh jūngyi tàahn gittā /gongkàhm.

I like the cinema. _____ 我鐘意睇戲。
                           Ngóh jūngyi tái hei.

I like traveling/playing ____ 我鐘意旅行／運動／釣魚／散步。
sports/going fishing/   Ngóh jūngyi léuihhàhng / wahnduhng / diuyú /
going for a walk   saanbouh.

3.7 Being the host(ess)

See also 4 Eating out

What would you like to ____ 你想飲啲乜嘢呀？
drink?   Néih séung yám dī mātyéh a?

Something non-alcoholic, 有冇啲飲嘢入邊冇酒精㗎？
please   Yáuh-móuh dī yámyéh yahpbihn móuh jáujīng
                           ga?

Would you like a _____ cigarette/cigar?	你想唔想食枝煙／雪茄呀？ Néih séung-m̀h-séung sihk jī yīn/syutgā a?
I don't smoke _____	我唔食煙嘅。 Ngóh m̀h'sihk-yīn ge.

3.8 Invitations

Are you doing anything tonight?	今晚你想做啲乜嘢呀？ (informal) Gāmmáahn néih séung jouh mātyéh a? 今晚你安排咗乜嘢活動呀？ (formal) Gāmmáahn néih ngōnpàaih-jó mātyéh wuhtduhng a?
Do you have any plans for today/this afternoon/ tonight?	今日／下晝／夜晚你有乜嘢安排／活動？ Gāmyaht/hahjau/yehmáahn néih yáuh mātyéh ngōnpàaih/wuhtduhng?
Would you like to go out with me?	我哋出街行吓，好嗎？ (formal) Ngóhdeih chēut-gāai hàahng-háh, hóu ma? 有冇興趣出街行呀？ (informal) Yáuh-móuh hingcheui chēut-gāai hàahng a?
Would you like to go dancing with me?	我哋去跳舞，好嗎？ (formal) Ngóhdeih heui tiu-móuh, hóu ma? 有冇興趣去跳舞呀？ (informal) Yáuh-móuh hingcheui heui tiu-móuh a?
Would you like to have lunch/dinner with me?	我哋出去食晏／晚飯，好嗎？ (formal) Ngóhdeih chēut-heui sihk ngaan/ máahnfaahn, hóu ma? 有冇興趣出街食晏／晚飯呀？ (informal) Yáuh-móuh hingcheui chēut-gāai sihk ngaan/máahnfaahn a?
Would you like to come to the beach with me?	我哋去海灘玩，好嗎？ (formal) Ngóhdeih heui hóitāan wáan*, hóu ma? 有冇興趣同我去海灘玩呀？ (informal) Yáuh-móuh hingcheui tùhng ngóh heui hóitāan wáan* a?
Would you like to come into town with us?	我哋入城玩，好嗎？ (formal) Ngóhdeih yahp-séng* wáan*, hóu ma? 有冇興趣同我入城玩呀？ (informal) Yáuh-móuh hingcheui tùhng ngóh yahp-séng* wáan* a?
Would you like to come and see some friends with us?	我哋去探朋友，你想唔想一齊嚟呀？ (formal) Ngóhdeih heui taam pàhngyáuh, néih séung-m̀h-séung yātchàih làih a? 有冇興趣同我哋一齊去探朋友呀？ (informal) Yáuh-móuh hingcheui tùhng ngóhdeih yātchàih heui taam pàhngyáuh a?
Shall we dance?	我哋跳舞，好唔好呀？ Ngóhdeih tiu-móuh, hóu-m̀h-hóu a?
– sit at the bar?	去酒巴坐吓？ Heui jáubā chóh-háh?
– get something to drink?	飲啲乜嘢呀？ Yám dī mātyéh a?

– go for a walk? _____	出去行吓，好唔好呀？
	Chēut-heui hàahng-háh, hóu-m̀h-hóu a?
– go for a drive? _____	去遊車河，好唔好呀？
	Heui yàuhchēhó, hóu-m̀h-hóu a?
Yes, all right ___ _____	好呃！
	Hóu ak!
Good idea _____	好主意！
	Hóu jyúyi!
No, thank you _____	唔好喇，多謝嘞！
	M̀h'hóu la, dōjeh laak.
Maybe later. _____	遲啲先啦。
	Chìh-dī sīn lā.
I don't feel like it. _____	我冇心情。
	Ngóh móuh sāmchìhng.
I don't have time. _____	我唔得閒。
	Ngóh m̀h'dākhàahn.
I already have a date. _____	我已經約咗人。
	Ngóh yíging yeuk-jó yàhn.
I'm not very good at _____	我唔係好識跳舞／打排球／遊水。
dancing/volleyball/	Ngóh m̀h'haih hóu sīk tiu-móuh / dá pàaihkàuh
swimming	/ yàuh-séui.

.9 Paying a compliment

You look great! _____	你睇起嚟真神氣！
	Néih tái-héi-làih jān sàhnhei!
I like your car! _____	你架車真係正！
	Néih ga chē jānhaih jeng!
I like your ski outfit! _____	你件滑雪裝真係正！
	Néih gihn waahtsyut-jōng jānhaih jeng!
You are very nice _____	你對人真好！／妳真係好人！
(formal/informal)	Néih deui yàhn jān hóu! / Néih jan haih hóuyàhn!
What a good boy/girl! _____	呢個細蚊仔真乖！
	Nī go saimanjái jān gwāai.
You're a good dancer. _____	你跳舞跳得好靚。
	Néih tiu-móuh tiu-dāk hóu leng.
You're a very good cook. __	你煮餸煮得真係好味。
	Néih jyú-sung jyú-dāk jānhaih hóumeih.
You're a good soccer _____	你踢波踢得真係勁。
player.	Néih tek-bō tek-dāk jānhaih gihng.

.10 Intimate comments/questions

I like being with you. _____	我鐘意同你喺／響一齊。
	Ngóh jūngyi tùhng néih hái/héung yātchàih.
I've missed you so much __	我想你想得好苦。
	Ngóh séung néih séung-dāk hóu fú.
I dreamt about you. _____	我發夢都諗住你。
	Ngóh faatmuhng dōu nám-jyuh néih.
I think about you all day. __	我一日到黑都諗住你。
	Ngóh yāt-yaht-dou-hāk dōu nám-jyuh néih.

I've been thinking about you all day.	我成日都諗住你。 Ngóh sèhngyaht dōu nám-jyuh néih.
You have such a sweet smile.	你笑得真係甜。 Néih siu-dāk jānhaih tìhm.
You have such beautiful eyes	你對眼真係迷人。 Néih deui ngáahn jānhaih màih-yàhn.
I love you (I'm fond of you).	我鐘意你。 Ngóh jūngyi néih.
I'm in love with you.	我愛上你。 Ngóh ngoi-séuhng néih.
I'm in love with you too.	我都愛上你。 Ngóh dōu ngoi-séuhng néih.
I love you.	我愛你。 Ngóh ngoi néih.
I love you too.	我都愛你。 Ngóh dōu ngoi néih.
I don't feel as strongly about you.	我對你冇特別嘅感情。 Ngóh deui néih móuh dahkbiht ge gámchìhng.
I already have a girlfriend/boyfriend.	我已經有咗女／男朋友。 Ngóh yíhgīng yáuh-jó néuih'/nàahm'pàhngyáuh.
I'm not ready for that.	我對你嘅感情仲未到呢一步。 Ngóh deui néih ge gámchìhng juhng meih dou nī yāt bouh.
I don't want to rush into it.	我唔想咁快就嘅樣。 Ngóh m̀h'séung gam faai jauh gámyéung*.
Take your hands off me.	攞開你隻手！ Ló-hōi néih jek sáu!
Okay, no problem.	得，冇問題。 Dāk, móuh mahntàih.
Will you spend the night with me?	你肯唔肯陪我瞓一晚？ Néih háng-m̀h-háng pùih ngóh fan yāt máahn?
I'd like to go to bed with you.	我想同你瞓一晚。 Ngóh séung tùhng néih fan yāt máahn.
Only if we use a condom.	不過一定要用避孕套。 Bātgwo yātdihng yiu yuhng beihyahn-tou.
We have to be careful about AIDS.	我哋要小心愛滋病。 Ngóhdeih yiu síusām ngoijī-behng.
That's what they all say.	啲人都係噉話。 Dī yàhn dōu haih gám wah.
We shouldn't take any risks	我哋唔應該冒呢個險。 Ngóhdeih m̀h'yīnggōi mouh nī go hím.
Do you have a condom?	你有冇避孕套呀？ Néih yáuh-móuh beihyahn-tou a?
No? Then the answer's "no".	冇啊？冇就唔可以（性交）。 Móuh àh? Móuh jauh m̀h'hóyíh (singgāau).

3.11 Arrangements

When will I see you again?	我幾時再見到你？ Ngóh géisìh joi gin-dóu néih?

Are you (informal) free over the weekend?	呢個週末你得唔得閒？ Nī go jāumuht néih dāk-m̀h-dākhàahn?
What's the plan, then?	你有乜嘢計劃？ Néih yáuh mātyéh gaiwaahk?
Where shall we meet?	我哋喺／響邊度見面？ Ngóhdeih hái/héung bīndouh ginmihn?
Will you pick me/us up?	你係唔係嚟接我／我哋呀？ Néih haih-m̀h-haih làih jip ngóh/ngóhdeih a?
Shall I pick you up?	係唔係我嚟接你／你哋呀？ Haih-m̀h-haih ngóh làih jip néih/néihdeih a?
I have to be home by...	我…前一定要返到屋企。 Ngóh ...chìhn yātdihng yiu fāan-dou ngūkkéi.
I don't want to see you anymore.	我唔想再見到你。 Ngóh m̀h'séung joi gin-dóu néih.

3.12 Saying good-bye

Can I take you home?	我可以送你返屋企嗎？ Ngóh hóyíh sung néih fāan ngūkkéi* ma?
Can I write/call you?	我可以寫信／打電話俾你嗎？ Ngóh hóyíh sé-seun / dá-dihnwá* béi néih ma?
Will you write to me/ call me?	你會唔會寫信／打電話俾我呀？ Néih wúih-m̀h-wúih sé-seun / dá-dihnwá* béi ngóh a?
Can I have your address/phone number?	你可以俾你個地址／電話我嗎？ Néih hóyíh béi néih go deihjí/ dihnwá* ngóh ma?
Thanks for everything.	多謝你為我做嘅一切。 Dōjeh néih waih ngóh jouh ge yātchai.
It was a lot of fun.	我們玩得好開心。 Ngóhdeih wáan*-dāk hóu hōisāam.
Say hello to... (informal).	幫我問候…。 Bōng ngóh mahnhauh ...
All the best!	祝你萬事如意！ Jūk néih maahn sih yùh yi!
Good luck!	祝你好運！ Jūk néih hóuwahn!
When will you be back?	你幾時返嚟呀？ Néih géisìh fāan-làih a?
I'll be waiting for you.	我會等你返嚟。 Ngóh wúih dáng néih fāan-làih.
I'd like to see you again.	我想再見到你。 Ngóh séung joi gin-dóu néih.
I hope we meet again soon.	我希望好快就再見到你。 Ngóh hēimohng hóu faai jauh joi gin-dóu néih.
Here's my address. If you're ever in the United States	呢個係我嘅地址。第日你嚟美國， 一定要嚟搵我。 Nī go haih ngóh ge deihjí, daihyaht néih làih Méihgwok yātdihng yiu làih wán ngóh.
You'd be more than welcome.	你幾時嚟，我都好歡迎。 Néih géisìh làih, ngóh dōu hóu fūnyìhng.

Eating out

4.1 **O**n arrival 39

4.2 **O**rdering 40

4.3 **T**he bill 42

4.4 **C**omplaints 43

4.5 **P**aying a compliment 43

4.6 **R**equests 44

4.7 **D**rinks 45

4.8 **C**antonese yamcha 46

4.9 **C**antonese dishes 47

4.10 **W**estern dishes 47

4 Eating out

● **Foreigners visiting Hong Kong** generally take their meals in restaurants in their hotels or in nearby restaurants. Occasionally they are taken out to restaurants specialized in one type of cuisine, eg. Peking duck, Sichuan steamboat, Mongolian barbecues, Shanghai dumplings etc. In order to eat at most restaurants outside the hotels, it is necessary to make arrangements ahead of time.

Mealtimes

In Hong Kong people usually have three meals:
1. jóuchāan 早飯 (breakfast), is eaten sometime between 7.30 and 10:00 a.m. It generally consists of buns, eggs, assorted dimsims known collectively in the West as 'yamcha food', congee and fried cruller.
2. nghchāan/ngaanjau 午餐/晏晝 (lunch), eaten between 12:00 and 2.00 p.m., usually include a hot dish. School children eat in school canteens or in nearby restaurants. Lunch usually consists of rice or noodles with stir-fried meats or seafood on top.
3. máahnfaahn 晚飯 (dinner) is considered to be the most important meal of the day, at around 7:00 or 8:00 p.m. It often includes a clear soup and a few meat and vegetable dishes, and is usually taken with the family.

4.1 On arrival

I'd like to reserve a _____ table for seven o'clock, please	我想訂張七點嘅檯。 Ngóh séung dehng jēung chāt dím ge tói.
A table for two, please. _____	兩位，唔該。 Léuhng wái*, mh'gōi.
We've reserved. _____	我哋訂咗檯。 Ngóhdeih dehng-jó tói.
We haven't reserved. _____	我哋冇訂檯。 Ngóhdeih móuh dehng-tói.

你哋有冇訂檯呀? _____	Do you have a reservation?
你用乜嘢名訂檯㗎? _____	What name please?
請跟我過嚟呢邊。 _____	This way, please.
呢張檯已經有人訂咗。 _____	This table is reserved.
十五分鐘後就有一張空檯。 _____	We'll have a table free in fifteen minutes.
你介唔介意等一陣呀? _____	Would you mind waiting?

Is the restaurant open _____ yet?	餐廳開咗門未呀? Chāantēng hōi-jó mùhn meih a?
What time does the _____ restaurant open?	餐廳幾時開門呀? Chāantēng géisìh hōi-mùhn a?

What time does the restaurant close?	餐廳幾時閂門門？ Chāantēng géisìh sāan-mùhn?
Can we wait for a table?	如果我哋等一陣，有冇檯呀？ Yùhgwó ngóhdeih dáng yātjahn, yáuh-móuh tói a?
Do we have to wait long?	駛唔駛等好耐呀？ Sái-m̀h-sái dáng hóu noih a?
Is this seat taken?	呢個位有人坐嗎？ Nī go wái* yáuh yàhn chóh ma?
Could we sit here?	我哋可以坐喺／響呢度嗎？ Ngóhdeih hóyíh chóh hái/héung nīdouh ma?
Can we sit by the window?	我哋可以坐窗口位嗎？ Ngóhdeih hóyíh chóh chēungháu wái* ma?
Are there any tables outside?	出邊有冇空檯呀？ chēutbihn yáuh-móuh hūng tói a?
Do you have another chair for us?	唔該俾多張凳我哋吖。 M̀h'gōi béi dō jēung dang ngóhdeih ā.
Do you have a highchair?	唔該俾張高凳我哋吖。 M̀h'gōi béi jēung gōudang ngóhdeih ā.
Is there a socket for this bottle-warmer?	有冇插呢個暖瓶器嘅插蘇？ Yáuh-móuh chaap nī go nyúhnpìhng-hei ge chaapsōu?
Could you warm up this bottle/jar for me? (in the microwave)	唔該幫我用微波爐暖一下呢個奶樽。 M̀h'gōi bōng ngóh yuhng mèihbō-lòuh nyúhn yāt-háh nī go náaihjēun.
Not too hot, please	唔好太熱，唔該。 M̀h'hóu taai yiht, m̀h'gōi.
Is there somewhere I can change the baby's diaper?	有冇地方換 BB 仔尿布呀？ Yáuh-móuh deihfōng wuhn bìhbíjái niuhbou a?
Where are the restrooms?	洗手間喺／響邊度呀？ Sáisáu-gāan hái/héung bīndouh a?

4.2 Ordering

Waiter/Waitress!	伙記／侍應生／服務員！ Fógei/Sihyingsāng/fuhkmouh-yùhn!
Madam!	女士／太太／小姐！ néuihsih/taaitáai*/síujé!
Sir!	先生！ Sīnsāang!
We'd like something to eat/drink.	我哋想食／飲啲嘢。 Ngóhdeih séung sihk/yám dī yéh.
Could I have a quick meal?	有啲乜嘢餐係最快㗎？ Yáuhdī mātyéh chāan haih jeui faai ga?
We don't have much time.	我哋要趕時間。 Ngóhdeih yiu gón sìhgaan.
We'd like to have a drink first.	我哋想飲杯嘢先。 Ngóhdeih séung yám būi yéh sīn.
Could we see the menu/wine list, please?	唔該俾我哋睇吓菜牌／酒牌。 M̀h'gōi béi ngóhdeih tái-háh choipáai*/jáu'páai*.

Do you have a menu in English?	有冇英文嘅菜牌呀？ Yáuh-móuh Yīngmán* ge choipáai* a?
Do you have a dish of the day?	今日有冇特別嘅菜？ Gāmyaht yáuh-móuh dahkbiht ge choi?
Do you have a tourist menu?	有冇俾遊客食嘅菜牌？ Yáuh-móuh béi yàuhhaak sihk ge choipáai*?
We haven't made a choice yet.	我哋仲未諗到食乜嘢？ Ngóhdeih juhng meih nám-dóu sihk mātyéh.
What do you recommend?	唔該介紹啲好菜。 Mh'gōi gaaisiuh dī hóu choi.
What are the local specialities?	你哋有啲乜嘢風味菜呀？ Néihdeih yáuh dī mātyéh fūngmeih-choi a?
What are your specialities?	你哋有啲乜嘢招牌菜呀？ Néihdeih yáuh dī mātyéh jīupàaih-choi a?
I don't like meat/fish	我唔鐘意食肉／魚。 Ngóh mh'jūngyi sihk yuhk/yú.
What's this?	呢啲係乜嘢嚟㗎？ Nīdī haih mātyéh làihga?
Does it have...in it?	入邊有冇...？ Yahpbihn yáuh-móuh ... ?
What does it taste like?	乜嘢味道㗎？ Mātyéh meihdouh ga?
Is this a hot or a cold dish?	呢個菜熱定（係）凍㗎？ Nī go choi yiht dihng(haih) dung ga?
Is this sweet?	呢個菜係唔係甜㗎？ Nī go choi haih-mh-haih thm ga?
Is this hot/spicy?	呢個菜辣唔辣㗎？ Nī go choi laaht-mh-laaht ga?

（你／你哋）想食啲乜嘢呢？	What would you like?
（你／你哋）諗定食乜嘢未呀？	Have you decided?
（你／你哋）想唔想飲啲嘢先呀？	Would you like a drink first?
（你／你哋）飲啲乜嘢先呢？	What would you like to drink?
唔唔賣晒…	We've run out of ...
菜嚟齊喇，請。	Enjoy your meal.
飯菜做得好唔好食呀？	Is everything all right?
收得檯未呀？	May I clear the table?

Do you have anything else, by any chance?	仲有冇菜未嚟呀？ Juhng máuh-móuh choi meih làih a?
I'm on a salt-free diet.	我唔食得鹽。 Ngóh mh'sihk-dāk yìhm.
I can't eat pork.	我唔食得豬肉。 Ngóh mh'sihk-dāk jyūyuhk.
I can't have sugar.	我唔食得糖。 Ngóh mh'sihk-dāk tòhng.

Eating out

I'm on a fat-free diet.	我唔食得油膩嘅。 Ngóh m̀h'sihk-dāk yàuhneih ge.
I can't have spicy food.	我唔食得辣嘅／帶香料嘅菜。 Ngóh m̀h'sihk-dāk laaht ge / daai hēunglíu* ge choi.
We'll have what those people are having.	我哋要佢哋食嗰啲菜。 Ngóhdeih yiu kéihdeih sihk gó dī choi.
I'd like...	要一個... Yiu yāt go ...
We're not having Beijing Duck dish.	我哋唔要北京鴨。 Ngóhdeih m̀h'yiu Bākgīng-ngaap.
Could I have some more rice, please?	唔該俾多啲白飯。 M̀h'gōi béi dō-dī baahkfaahn.
Could I have another bottle of boiled water/ wine, please?	唔該俾多一樽礦泉水／酒。 M̀h'gōi béi dō yāt jēun kwongchyùhn-séui/ jáu.
Could I have another portion of..., please?	唔該俾多一個... M̀h'gōi béi dō yāt go ...
Could I have the salt and pepper, please?	唔該俾啲鹽同胡椒粉。 M̀h'gōi béi dī yìhm tùhng wùhjīufán.
Could I have a napkin, please?	唔該俾條餐巾我。 M̀h'gōi béi tìuh chāan'gān ngóh.
Could I have a teaspoon, please?	唔該俾個茶羹我。 M̀h'gōi béi go chàhgāng ngóh.
Could I have an ashtray, please?	唔該俾個煙灰盅我。 M̀h'gōi béi go yīnfūi-jūng ngóh.
Could I have some matches, please?	唔該俾盒火柴我。 M̀h'gōi béi hahp fóchàaih ngóh.
Could I have some toothpicks, please	唔該俾啲牙簽我。 M̀h'gōi béi dī ngàhchīm ngóh.
Could I have a glass of boiled water, please?	唔該俾杯滾水我。 M̀h'gōi béi būi gwánséui ngóh.
Could I have a straw please?	唔該俾枝飲筒我。 M̀h'gōi béi jī yámtúng ngóh.
Enjoy your meal.	菜嚟齊喇，請! Choi làih-chàih la, chíng!
Cheers!	飲勝! Yámsing!
The next round's on me.	下次我請。 Hah chi ngóh chéng.
Could we have a doggy bag, please?	唔該幫我打包。 M̀h'gōi bōng ngóh dábāau.

.3 The bill

See also 8.2 Settling the bill

How much is this dish?	呢碟菜幾多錢? Nī dihp choi géidō chín*?
Could I have the bill, please?	唔該埋單。 M̀h'gōi màaihdāan.

All together	總共... Júngguhng ....
Everyone pays separately	我哋各自埋單。 Ngóhdeih gokjih màaihdān.
Let's go Dutch.	我哋分咗呢張單佢。 Ngóhdeih fān-jó nī jēung dāan kéuih.
Could we have the menu again, please?	麻煩你俾個菜牌我哋。 Màhfàahn néih béi go choipáai* ngóhdeih.
The...is not on the bill.	張單上面冇呢個菜。 Jēungdāan seuhngmihn móuh nī go choi.

4.4 Complaints

It's taking a very long time.	我已經等咗好耐喇。 Ngóh yíhgīng dáng-jó hóu noih la.
We've been here an hour already.	我哋嚟咗已經一個鐘頭喇。 Ngóhdeih làih-jó yíhgīng yāt go jūngtàuh la.
This must be a mistake.	我諗你哋搞錯喇。 Ngóh nám néihdeih gáau-cho la.
This is not what I ordered.	我哋冇叫呢碟菜。 Ngóhdeih móuh giu nī dihp choi.
I ordered...	我叫嗰碟菜係... Ngóh giu gó dihp choi haih ...
There's a dish missing.	少咗一碟菜。 Síu-jó yāt dihp choi.
The plate is broken/not clean.	呢個碟崩咗 / 唔乾淨。 Nī go díp* bāng-jó / m̀h'gōnjehng.
The food's cold	呢碟菜凍咗。 Nī dihp choi dung-jó.
The food's not fresh.	呢碟菜唔新鮮。 Nī dihp choi m̀h'sānsīn.
The food's too salty/sweet/spicy.	呢碟菜太鹹 / 甜 / 辣喇。 Nī dihp choi taai hàahm/tìhm/laaht la.
The food is off/has gone bad.	呢碟菜有啲叔味。 Nī dihp choi yáuh dī sūk meih.
Could I have something else instead of this?	換碟第二啲嘅菜，得唔得呀？ Wuhn dihp daih-yih dī ge choi, dāk-m̀h-dāk a?
The bill/this amount is not right.	呢張單好似加錯咗。 Nī jēung dāan hóuchíh gā-cho-jó.
We didn't have this.	我哋冇叫呢碟菜。 Ngóhdeih móuh giu nī dihp choi.
There's no toilet paper in the restroom.	洗手間入邊冇廁紙。 Sáisáu-gāan yahpbihn móuh chíjí.
Will you call the manager, please?	唔該叫你哋嘅經理嚟。 M̀h'goi giu néihdeih ge gīngléih làih.

4.5 Paying a compliment

That was a sumptuous meal.	啲菜好豐富。 Dī choi hóu fūngfu.

The food was excellent.	啲菜煮得好食。	Dī choi jyú-dāk hóusihk.
The...in particular was delicious.	特別係..., 真係太好食喇。	Dahkbiht haih ..., jānhaih taai hóusihk la.

4.6 Requests

Please give me	唔該俾我...	Mh'gōi béi ngóh ...
the menu	餐牌 / 菜牌	chāanpáai*/choipáai*
a pair of chopsticks	一對筷子	yāt deui faaijí
a fork	一個叉	yāt go chā
a knife	一把刀	yāt bá dōu
a plate	一個碟	yāt go díp*
a bowl	一個碗	yāt go wún
a spoon	一個匙羹	yāt go chìhgāng
salt	鹽	yìhm
pepper	胡椒粉	wùhjīu-fán
sugar	糖	tòhng
starter/hors d'oeuvre	餐前小食	chāanchìhn síusihk
fruit	生果	sāanggwó
ice cream	雪糕	syutgōu
meat	肉	yuhk
salad	沙律	sāleut*/sāleut*
main course	正餐	jingchāan
side dishes/vegetables	配菜 / 蔬菜	puichoi/sōchoi
service charge (included)	貼士 (已包括在內)	tīpsí (yíh bāaukut joih noih)
soup	湯	tōng
specialities	特色菜	dahksīk-choi
breakfast	早餐	jóuchāan

lunch	午餐 nghchāan
dinner	晚餐 / 晚飯 máahnchāan/máahnfaahn
snacks	小食 síusihk
bread	麵包 mihnbāau
cakes/desserts	蛋糕 / 甜品 daahn'gōu/tìhmbán
noodles	麵 mihn
vegetables	蔬菜 sōchoi
cheese	芝士 jīsí
fish	魚 yú
pizza	薄餅 bohkbéng
McDonald's hamburger	漢堡包 hōnbóu-bāau
Kentucky Fried Chicken	炸雞 jagāi

 .7 Drinks

coffee	咖啡 gāfēi
hot/cold cocoa	熱 / 凍朱古力 yiht/dung jyūgūlīk
hot/cold milk	熱 / 凍牛奶 yiht/dung ngàuhnáaih
black tea	紅茶（唔加奶） hùhngchàh (m̀h'gā náaih)
English tea (with milk)	奶茶 náaihchàh
jasmine tea	香片 hēungpín*
beer	啤酒 bējáu
orange juice	橙汁 cháangjāp
freshly squeezed orange juice	鮮榨橙汁 sīnjā-cháangjāp
mineral water	礦泉水 kwongchyùhn-séui
soda water	梳打水 sōdá-séui

coca cola	可口可樂	hóháu'hólohk
brandy	白蘭地	baahklāandéi*
whisky	威士忌	wāisihgéi
champagne	香檳	hēungbān
red wine	紅葡萄酒	hùhng pòuhtòuh-jáu
white wine	白葡萄酒	baahk pòuhtòuh-jáu

4.8 Cantonese yamcha

● **The Cantonese word** yámchàh (飲茶) literarally means 'drink tea' but implies having a Cantonese dimsim meal. Pronounced sihk dímsām (食點心), this type of meal is served from early morning to early afternoon along with tea as the main beverage and consists of very small portions of snack foods. The food is pushed along on carts, and you simply signal the waitress when you wish a dish of whatever's just come by. The idea of a dimsim meal is to nibble on many different types of delicacies in a single sitting.

We are a party of eight	我哋八位。	Ngóhdeih baat wái*
Please bring us a pot of ... tea.	唔該俾一壺...茶。	Mh'gōi béi yāt wùh ... chàh. ...
Po'nei (Yunnan tea)	普洱	póu'néi
Jasmine	香片	hēungpín*
Po'nei with chrysanthemum	菊普	gūkpóu
saumei	壽眉	sauhméi*
Please give me a plate of ...	唔該俾一碟...	Mh'gōi béi yāt dihp ...
prawn dumplings	蝦餃	hāgáau
open-topped steamed pork dumplings	燒賣	sīumáai*
barbecued pork buns	叉燒包	chāsīu-bāau
spring rolls	春卷	chēun'gyún
deep-fried taro root dimsim	芋角	wuhgók*
steamed stuffed rice crepes	腸粉	chéung*fán
spareribs in black bean sauce	豉汁排骨	sihjāp-pàaihgwāt

steamed beef balls with beancurd skin	山竹牛肉 sāanjūk ngàuhyuhk
glutinous rice with meat stuffed in lotus leaves	糯米雞 nohmáih-gāi
turnip cake	蘿蔔糕 lòhbaahk-gōu
Chinese green vegetables	油菜 yàuhchoi
egg tarts	蛋撻 daahntāat
jellied beancurd	豆腐花 dauhfuhfā
braised beef with rice noodles	乾炒牛河 gōncháau ngàuhhó*

4.9 Cantonese dishes

Cantonese dishes	廣東菜 Gwóngdūng-choi
assorted cold dishes	拼盤 pingpún*
hot and sour seafood soup	酸辣湯 syūnlaaht-tōng
sweet and sour pork	咕嚕肉 Gúlóuh-yuhk
deep-fried (spring) chicken	炸子雞 jají-gāi
saute beef with onion	洋葱炒牛肉 Yèuhngchūng cháo ngàuhyuhk
saute fresh mushroom and choisam	香菇菜心 Hēunggū choisām
saute bean-curd with brown sauce	紅燒豆腐 Hùhngsīu dauhfuh
sauteed fresh scallops	油泡帶子 yàuhpaau daaijí
fried rice with eggs	炒飯 cháaufaahn

4.10 Western dishes

Western dishes	西餐 Sāichāan
soft boiled egg	煮雞蛋 jyú gāidáan*
scrambled egg	炒雞蛋 cháau gāidáan*
sandwich	三文治 sāammàhnjih
butter	牛油 ngàuhyàuh

On the road

5.1 **A**sking for directions   49

5.2 **L**uggage   50

5.3 **T**raffic signs   51

5.4 **T**he car   51
The parts of a car   *52-53*

5.5 **T**he gas station   54

5.6 **B**reakdown and repairs   54

5.7 **T**he bicycle/moped   58
*The parts of a
bicycle*   *56-57*

5.8 **R**enting a bicycle/
moped   58

5.9 **H**itchhiking   59

5 **On** the road

5.1 **A**sking for directions

Excuse me, could I ask you something?	對唔住，我可以問你啲嘢嗎？ Deui'mh-jyuh, ngóh hóyíh mahn néih dī yéh ma?
I've lost my way	我蕩失咗。 Ngóh dohng-sāt-jó.
Is there a ... around here?	附近有冇…？ Fuhgahn yáuh-móuh ... ?
Excuse me, what direction is ...?	請問，…喺/響邊個方向？ Chíngmahn, ... hái/héung bīn go fōngheung?
Excuse me, am I going in the right direction for ...?	請問，去…係唔係行呢個方向呀？ Chíngmahn, heui .... haih-mh-haih hàahng nī go fōngheung a?
bus stop	巴士站 bāsí-jaahm
railway station	火車站 fóchē-jaahm
subway station	地鐵站 deihtit-jaahm
Could you tell me how to get to...?	請問，…點去呀？ Chíngmahn, ... dím heui a?
How many kilometers is it to...?	去…有幾多公里呀？ heui ... yáuh géidō gūngléih a?
Is it far?	遠唔遠呀？ Yúhn-mh-yúhn a?
Can I walk there?	行唔行到去呀？ Hàahng-mh-hàahng-dóu heui a?
Is it difficult to find?	容唔容易搵呀？ Yùhng-mh-yùhngyih wán a?

唔清楚喎，我呢度啲路唔熟。	I don't know, I don't know my way around here
你行錯咗喇。	You're going the wrong way
你要行返轉頭。	You have to go back
由呢度開始，跟住路牌行。	From there on just follow the signs
到咗之後再問人。	When you get there, ask again
一直行。	Go straight ahead
行到盡頭。	Go till end of road
跟住	Follow
過	Cross

轉右	Turn right
轉左	Turn left
路 / 街	the road/street
河	the river
紅綠燈 / 交通燈	the traffic light
高架橋	the overpass
隧道	the tunnel
橋	the bridge
鐵路同公路嘅交叉口	the grade crossing
樓	the building
路牌	the signs pointing to
街口 / 角落頭	at the corner
箭嘴	the arrow
十字路口	the intersection/cross-roads

5.2 Luggage

Porter!	搬運員! Būnwahn-yùhn!
Could you take this luggage to...?	唔該幫我將行李搬去... M̀h'gōi bōng ngóh jēung hàhngléih būn-heui ...
This is a small tip for you.	呢度少少貼士係俾你嘅。 Nīdouh síusíu tīpsí* haih béi néih ge.
Where can I find a cart?	邊度有手推車? Bīndouh yáuh sáutēui-chē?
Could you store this luggage for me.	唔該幫我存放呢件行李。 M̀h'gōi bōng ngóh chyùhnfong nē gin hàhngléih.
Where are the luggage lockers?	行李櫃喺 / 響邊度呀? Hàhngléih-gwaih hái/héung bīndouh a?
I can't get the locker open.	我開唔到行李櫃。 Ngóh hōi-m̀h-dóu hàhngléih-gwaih.
How much is it per item per day?	存放一件行李一日要幾多錢? Chyùhnfong yāt gihn hàhngléih yāt yaht géidō chín*?
This is not my bag/suitcase.	呢個唔係我嘅旅行袋 / 皮夾。 Nī go m̀h'haih ngóh ge léuihhàhng-dói* / pèihgīp.
There's one item/bag/suitcase missing.	我唔見咗一個旅行袋 / 皮夾。 Ngóh m̀h'gin-jó yāt go léuihhàhng-dói* / pèihgīp.
My suitcase is damaged.	我個皮夾俾人整壞咗。 Ngóh go pèihgīp béi yàhn jíng-waaih-jó.

5.3 Traffic signs

交通訊號 Traffic signs	不能通行嘅路肩 unpassable shoulder	繞道行駛 detour
入隧道請開着車頭燈。 turn on headlights (in the tunnel)	收費泊車 / 專用車位 paying carpark/ parking reserved for	下一段路多雨或雪 rain or ice for …kms
十字路口 intersection/ crossroads	靠右 / 左行駛 keep right/left	不準乘搭他人便車 no hitchhiking
汽車故障服務處。 road assistance (breakdown service)	小心山上滑落石頭 beware, falling rocks	(必須顯示)泊車票 parking disk (compulsory)
停(車) stop	監控停車場 supervised garage/ parking lot	優先使用車道權 right of way
安全島 / 行人道 traffic island/ pedestrian walk	道路阻塞 road blocked	不準轉右 / 左 no right/left turn
限時停車 parking for a limited period	換車道 change lanes	不準駛入 no entry
電油站 service station	(鐵路、公路)交叉口 grade crossing	慢駛 slow down
不準堵塞 do not obstruct	道路封閉 road closed	圓盤地帶 disk zone
路面損壞 / 不平 broken/uneven surface	淨空高度 maximum clearance	不準超車 no passing
小心 beware	出口 exit	不準泊車 no parking
前面修路 road works	緊急車道 emergency lane	單程路 one way
路不開放 road closed	車道口 driveway	停車被拖走地帶 tow-away area (both sides of the road)
載重貨車 heavy trucks	最高速度 maximum speed	優先使用車道權在路尾 right of way at end of road
通行費 toll payment	前面急彎 curves ahead	不準駛入 no entry
前面路窄 narrowing in the road	危險 danger(ous)	隧道 tunnel
	此路不通 / 行人不準通過 no access/ no pedestrian access	

5.4 The car

See the diagram on page 53

● Particular traffic regulations:

The speed limits for different vehicles vary in different cities and on different roads. Generally speaking for cars and motorcycles, 110 km/h on non-urban highways and 40 km/h on main roads and built-up areas. Otherwise speed limits on certain roads are clearly marked. Bicycles are not allowed to travel on highways but they are commonplace in the New Territories where special cycle lanes are provided. Unlike China, vehicles in Hong Kong have right-hand drive and travel on the left side of the road.

5

On the road

The parts of a car

(the diagram shows the numbered parts)

1	battery	電池	dihnchìh
2	rear light	尾燈	méihdāng
3	rear-view mirror	倒後鏡	dou'hauh-geng
	backup light	後備燈	hauhbeih-dāng
4	aerial	天線	tīnsin
	car radio	收音機	shāuyām-gēi
5	gas tank	油箱	yàuhsēung
6	spark plugs	火嘴	fójéui
	fuel pump	燃料泵	yìhnlíu*-bāng
7	side mirror	左 / 右倒後鏡	jó/yauh dou'hauh-geng
8	bumper	防撞杠 / 泵把	fòhngjohng-gōn/bāngbá
	carburettor	化油器	fayàuh-hei
	crankcase	曲柄軸箱	kūkbeng juhksēung
	cylinder	汽缸	heigōng
	ignition	士撻	sihtaat
	warning light	壞車燈	waaihchē-dāng
	generator	發電機	faatdihn-gēi
	accelerator	油門	yáu*mùhn
	handbrake	手掣	sáujai
	valve	活門	wuhtmùhn
9	muffler	滅聲器 / 死氣鼓	mihtsēng-hei/séihei-gú
10	trunk	車尾箱	chēméih-sēung
11	headlight	車頭燈	chētàuh-dāng
	crank shaft	曲軸	kūkjuhk
12	air filter	氣隔	heigaak
	fog lamp	霧燈	mouhdāng
13	engine block	車頭	chētáu*
	camshaft	凸輪軸	dahtléun*juhk
	oil filter/pump	油隔 / 濾油泵	yàuhgaak/leuihyàuh-bāng
	dipstick	油尺	yàuh-chek
	pedal	脚掣	geukjai
14	door	車門	chēmùhn
15	radiator	水箱	séuisēung
16	brake disc	碟形煞車掣	dihpyìhng saatchē-jai
	spare wheel	士啤呔	sihbē-tāai
17	indicator	右 / 左嶄燈	yauh/jó jáamdāng
18	windshield	擋風玻璃	dóngfūng bōlēi
	wiper	水撥	séuibuht
19	shock absorbers	避震器	beihjang-hei
	sunroof	天窗	tīnchēung
	spoiler	定風翼	dihngfūng-yihk
20	steering column	鈦盤座	táaihpùhn-joh
	steering wheel	鈦盤	táaihpùhn
21	exhaust pipe	死氣喉	séihei-hàuh
22	seat belt	安全帶	ngōnchyùhn-dáai*
	fan	風扇	fūngsin
23	distributor	錶板	bīubáan
	cables	威也	wāiyá*
24	gear shift	波鑭	bōdong

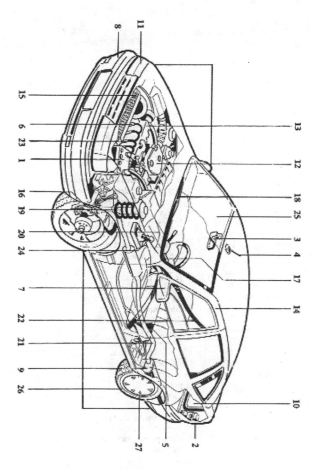

25	windshield	擋風玻璃	dóngfūng bōlēi
	water pump	水泵	séuibāng
26	wheel	車轆	chēlūk
27	hubcap	車轆襟	chēlūk-kám*
	piston	活塞	wuhtsāk
25	windshield	擋風玻璃	dǎngfēng bōli
	water pump	水泵	séuibāng
26	wheel	車輪	chēlún
27	hubcap	輪蓋	léun'goi
	piston	活塞	wuhtsāk

5.5 The gas station

● **The cost of gas in Hong Kong** in 2002 for Premium unleaded petrol is HKD11.00/liter, Standard unleaded petrol is HKD10.00 and leaded petrol is HKD12.50/liter, and diesel is HKD7.50/litre. LPG are mainly used by taxis and minibuses.

How many kilometers to the next gas station, please?	到下個電油站有幾遠？ Dou hah go dihnyàuh-jaahm yáuh géi yúhn?
I would like...litres of	我入...公升 Ngóh yahp .... gūngsīng
Premium unleaded petrol	超級無鉛電油 chīukāp mòuhyùhn dihnyàuh
Standard unleaded petrol	無鉛電油 mòuhyùhn dihnyàuh
– leaded petrol	含鉛電油 hàhm'yùhn dihnyàuh
– LPG gas	煤氣 mùihhei
– diesel	柴油 / 油渣 chàaihyàuh/yàuhjā
... dollars worth of gas	...蚊嘅電油 ...mān ge dihnyàuh
Fill her up, please	入滿佢，唔該 Yahp-múhn kéuih, m̀h'gōi.
Could you check...?	唔該幫我檢查一吓 M̀h'gōi bōng ngóh gímchàh yāt-háh.... .
– the oil level	機油 gēiyáu*
– the tire pressure	車呔 chētāai
Could you change the oil, please?	唔該幫我換機油 M̀h'gōi bōng ngóh wuhn gēiyáu*.
Could you clean the windshield, please?	唔該幫我擦乾淨擋風玻璃。 M̀h'gōi bōng ngóh chaat gōnjehng dóngfūng bōlēi.
Could you wash the car, please?	唔該幫我洗吓架車。 M̀h'gōi bōng ngóh sái-háh ga chē.

5.6 Breakdown and repairs

I have broken down, could you give me a hand?	我架車壞咗，可以幫一幫我嗎？ Ngóh ga chē waaih-jó, hóyíh bōng-yāt-bōng ngóh ma?
I have run out of gas	我架車冇晒電油。 Ngóh ga chē móuh-saai dihnyàuh.
I've locked the keys in the car	我將鎖匙鎖咗喺車入邊。 Ngóh jēung sósìh só-jó hái chē yahpbihn.
The car/motorbike won't start	我架車 / 電單車撻唔著火。 Ngóh ga chē/dihndāam-chē tāat-m̀h'jeuhk fó.

Could you contact the breakdown service for me, please?	唔該幫我打電話叫緊急服務。 Mh'gōi bōng ngóh dá-dihnwá* giu gán'gāp fuhkmouh.
Could you call a garage for me, please?	唔該幫我打電話搵車房師傅。 Mh'gōi bōng ngóh dá-dihnwá* wán chēfòhng sīfú*.
Could you give me a lift to...?	你可唔可以送我到...? Néih hó-mh-hóyíh sung ngóh dou ... ?
– to the nearest garage?	最近嘅車房? jeuikáhn ge chēfòhng?
– to the nearest telephone booth?	最近嘅公共電話亭? jeuikáhn ge gūngguhng dihnwá* tìhng?
– to the nearest emergency phone?	最近嘅緊急電話? jeuikáhn ge gán'gāp dihnwá*?
Can we take my motorcycle?	你可以運我架電單車嗎? Néih hóyíh wahn ngóh ga dihndāan-chē ma?
Could you tow me to a garage?	可唔可以拖我架車去車房呀? Hó-mh-hóyíh tō ngóh gā chē heui chēfòhng a?
There's probably something wrong with...(See 5.5)	...可能有啲壞。 ... hó'nàhng yáuh dī waaih
Can you fix it?	整唔整番呀? Jíng mh jíng-dāk-fāan a?
Could you fix my tire?	唔該幫我補呔。 Mh'gōi bōng ngóh bóu-tāai.
Could you change this wheel?	唔該幫我換個車轆。 Mh'gōi bong ngóh wuhn go chēlūk.
Can you fix it so it'll get me to ?	唔該幫我修理一下, 我要揸去... Mh'gōi bōng ngóh sāuléih-yāt-háh, ngóh yiu jā heui ...
Which garage can help me?	邊間車房可以幫到我呀? Bīn gāan chēfòhng hóyíh bōng-dóu* ngóh a?
When will my car/bicycle be ready?	我架車 / 電單車幾時整好呀? Ngóh ga chē / dihndāan-chē géisìh jíng-hóu a?
Have you already finished?	整好未呀? Jíng-hóu meih a?
Can I wait for it here?	我可以喺 / 響 (呢) 度等你整嗎? Ngóh hóyíh hái/héung (nī)douh dáng néih jíng ma?
How much will it cost?	要幾多錢呀? Yiu géidō chín* a?
Could you itemize the bill?	唔該你列出要修理嘅項目。 Mh'gōi néih liht-chēut yiu sāuléih ge hohngmuhk.
Could you give me a receipt for insurance purposes?	唔該俾張收據我做保險用途。 Mh'gōi béi jēung sāugeui ngóh jouh bóuhím yuhngtòuh.

On the road

The parts of a bicycle
(the diagram shows the numbered parts)

1	rear light	尾燈	méihdāng
2	rear wheel	後轆	hauhlūk
3	(luggage) carrier	行李籃	hàhngléih-láam*
4	fork	輪叉	léun*chā
5	bell	鐘	jūng
	inner tube	車膽	chēdáam
	tire	呔	tāai
6	peddle crank	腳踏曲柄	geukdaahp kūkbeng
7	gear change	變速器	bihnchūk-hei
	wire	威也	wāiyá*
	generator	發電機	faatdihn-gēi
	bicycle trailer	拖載單車嘅拖車	tōjoi dāanchē ge tōchē
	frame	車架	chēgá*
8	wheel guard	沙板	sābáan
9	chain	單車鏈	dāanchē-lín*
	chain guard	鏈嘁	lín*kám
	odometer	咪表	māibīu
	child's seat	小童座位	síutùhng johwái*
10	headlight	車頭燈	chētàuh-dāng
	bulb	燈膽	dāngdáam
11	pedal	腳掣	geukjai
12	pump	氣泵	heibāng
13	reflector	反光鏡	fáan'gwōng-geng
14	brake shoe	煞車皮	saatchē-péi*
15	brake cable	煞車威也	saatchē-wāiyá*
16	anti-theft device	防盜裝置	fòhngdouh jōngji
17	carrier straps	運載布帶	wahnjoi boudáai*
	tachometer	速度計	chūkdouh-gai
18	spoke	鋼線	gongsín*
19	mudguard	沙板	sābáan
20	handlebar	單車把手 / 鈦	dāanchē-básáu / táaih
21	chain wheel	齒輪	chílèuhn
	toe clip	腳踏扣	geukdaahp-kau
22	crank axle	曲柄軸	kūkbeng-juhk
	drum brake	鼓煞車	gú-saatchē
23	rim	車呔環	chētāai-wàahn
24	valve	活門	wuhtmùhn
25	gear cable	波箱威也	bōsēung wāiyá*
26	fork	輪叉	lèuhnchā
27	front wheel	前轆	chìhnlūk
28	seat	座位	johwái*

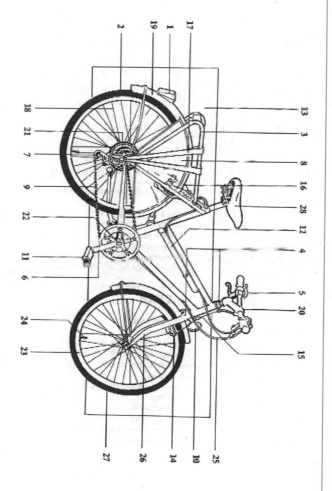

See the diagram on page 57

我冇你要嘅零件。	I don't have the parts that you want.
我要去第度幫你配零件。	I have to get the parts from somewhere else.
需要半日時間。	That'll take half a day.
需要一日時間。	That'll take a day.
需要幾日時間。	That'll take a few days.
需要一個星期 / 禮拜嘅時間。	That'll take a week.
修理費超過車 / 單車嘅本值。	Your car/bicycle is a write-off
你架車 / 電單車 / 單車整唔番。	It can't be repaired.
你架車 / 電單車 / 電動單車 / 單車...點就整好。	The car/motor bike/ moped/bicycle will be ready at... o'clock

5.8 **R**enting a bicycle/moped

I'd like to rent a...	我想租一架… Ngóh séung jōu yāt ga ...
Do I need a (special) license for that?	我駛唔駛要特別嘅車牌呀? Ngóh sái-m̀h-sái yiu dahkbiht ge chēpàaih a?
I'd like to rent the...	我想租… Ngóh séung jōu ...
for a day	一日… yāt yaht
for two days	兩日… léuhng yaht
How much is that per day/week?	租金一日 / 星期要幾多錢呀? Jōugām yāt yaht / sīngkèih yiu géidō chín* a?
How much is the deposit?	按金要幾多錢呀? Ngon'gām yiu géidō chín* a?
Could I have a receipt for the deposit?	唔該俾張按金收據我。 M̀h'gōi béi jēung ngon'gām sāugeui ngóh?
Does that include insurance?	(收費) 包括保險費嗎? (Sāufei) bāaukut bóuhím-fai ma?
What time can I pick the...up?	我幾時可以嚟攞車? Ngóh géisìh hóyíh làih ló-chē?
When does the...have to be back?	幾時要還車? Géisìh yiu wàahn-chē?
Where's the gas tank?	油箱喺 / 響邊度呀? Yàuhsēung hái/héung bīndouh a?
What sort of fuel does it take?	用乜嘢燃料㗎? Yuhng mātyéh yìhnlíu* ga?

Where are you heading?	你去邊個方向呀?
	Néih heui bīn go fōngheung a?
Can you give me a lift?	可唔可以搭你架車去呀?
	Hó-m̀h-hóyíh daap néih ga chē heui a?
Can my friend come too?	我朋友可唔可以嚟埋呀?
	Ngóh pàhngyáuh hó-m̀h-hóyíh làih-màaih a?
I'd like to go to...	我想去…
	Ngóh séung heui ...
Is that on the way to...?	呢條路係唔係去…?
	Nī tìuh louh haih-m̀h-haih heui ... ?
Could you drop me off...?	你可唔可以喺 / 響…停低我呀?
	Néih hó-m̀h-hóyíh hái/héung ... tìhng-dāi ngóh a?
Could you drop me off here?	你可唔可以喺 / 響呢度停低我呀?
	Néih hó-m̀h-hóyíh hái/héung nīdouh tìhng-dāi ngóh a?
– at the entrance to the highway?	喺 / 響公路嘅入口
	hái/héung gūnglouh ge yahp'háu
– in the center?	喺 / 響公路中間
	hái/héung gūnglouh jūnggāan
– at the next intersection?	喺 / 響下個十字路口
	hái/héung hah go sahpjih-louhháu
Could you stop here, please?	你可唔可以喺 / 響呢度停呀?
	Néih hó-m̀h-hóyíh hái nīdouh tìhng a?
I'd like to get out here	我想喺 / 響呢度落車。
	Ngóh séunghéung hái nīdouh lohk-chē.
Thanks for the lift	好多謝你俾我搭你架車!
	Hóu dōjeh néih béi ngóh daap néih ga chē!

On the road

59

Public transportation

6.1 In general   61

6.2 Questions to passengers   62

6.3 Tickets   63

6.4 Information   63

6.5 Airplanes   65

6.6 Long-distance trains   65

6.7 Taxis   66

6 Public transportation

6.1 In general

● **Public transport** is very efficient and accessible in Hong Kong. Ordinary people commute by subway, trains, buses, trams and ferries across from both sides of the harbor using 3 cross-harbor tunnels. In addition, there are mini-buses and taxis and a light rail system in the New Territories, so there is no real need for private cars. For example, the airport is well-serviced by the airport express, air-conditioned buses, taxis and ferries.

Where does this train go to?	呢班火車去邊度呀? Nī bāan fóchē heui bīndouh a?
Does this boat go to ... ?	呢隻船係唔係去...呀? Nī jek syùhn haih-m̀h-haih heui ... a?
Can I take this bus to ... ?	可唔可以坐呢架巴士去...呀? Hó-m̀h-hóyíh chóh nī ga bāsí heui ... a?
Does this train stop at ... ?	呢班火車停唔停...呀? Nī bāan fóchē tìhng-m̀h-tìhng ... a?
Is this seat taken/free/reserved?	呢個位有冇人坐呀? Nī go wái* yáuh-móuh yàhn chóh a?
I've reserved	我預定咗... Ngóh yuh-dehng-jó ...
Could you tell me where I have to get off for ...	去 ... 喺 / 響邊度落車呀? Heui ... hái/héung bīndouh lohk-chē a?
Could you let me know when we get to ...	到...唔該話俾我知。 Dou ... m̀h'gōi wah bēi ngóh jī.
Could you stop at the next stop, please?	唔該下個站有落。 M̀h'gōi hah go jaahm yáuh lohk.
Where are we?	我哋而家喺 / 響邊度呀? Ngóhdeih yìhgā hái/héung bīndouh a?
Do I have to get off here?	我係唔係響呢度落車呀? Ngóh haih-m̀h-haih héung nīdouh lohk chē a?
Have you already passed ...?	我哋過咗 ... 未呀? Ngóhdeih gwo-jó ... meih a?
How long have does this train stop here?	呢班火車會喺 / 響呢度停幾耐呀? Nī bāan fóchē wúih hái/héung nīdouh tìhng géi noih a?
Can I come back on the same ticket?	可唔可以用呢張飛坐返嚟呀? Hó-m̀h-hóyíh yuhng nī jēung fēi chóh fāan-làih a?
Can I change on this ticket?	我可唔可以用呢張飛轉車呀? Ngóh hó-m̀h-hóyíh yuhng nī jēung fēi jyun-chē a?
How long is this ticket valid for?	呢張飛可以用幾耐呀? Nī jēung fēi hóyíh yuhng géi noih a?

Ticket types

Single or return?	單程定係來回?
	Dāanchìhng dihnghaih lòihwùih?
Smoking or non-smoking?	吸煙車廂定係無煙車廂?
	Kāpyīn chēsēung dihnghaih mòuhyīn-chēsēung?
Window seat?	窗口位?
	Chēungháu-wái*?
Front or back (of train)?	(火車) 前邊定係後邊?
	(Fóchē) chìhngbihn dihnghaih hauhbihn?
Seat or berth?	座位定係臥舖?
	Johwái* dihnghaih ngohpōu?
How many are traveling?	有幾位乘客?
	Yáuh géi wái* sìhnghaak?

Destination

Where are you traveling?	你去邊度呀?
	Néih heui bīndouh a?
When are you leaving?	你幾時走呀?
	Néih géisìh jáu a?
Your train leaves at ...	你班火車 ... 點開車?
	Néih bāan fóchē ... dím hōi-chē.
You have to change.	你要換車
	Néih yiu wuhn-chē.
You have to get off at ...	你要喺 / 響... 落車
	Néih yiu hái/héung... lohk-chē.
You have to go via ...	你要經 ... 去 ...
	Néih yiu gīng ... heui ...
The outward journey is on ...	去程喺 / 響 ...
	Heuichìhng hái/héung ...
The return journey is on ...	回程喺 / 響 ...
	Wùihchìhng hái/héung ...
You have to on board by ... (o'clock)	你要喺 / 響 ... 點之前上車 / 機
	Néih yiu hái/héung ... dím jīchìhn séuhng-chē/gēi.

Inside the vehicle

Tickets, please	車飛吖, 唔該。
	Chēfēi ā, Mh'gōi.
Your reservation, please	唔該俾我睇吓你張訂飛單。
	Mh'gōi béi ngóh tái-háh néih jēung dehng-fēi-dāan.
Your passport, please	唔該俾我睇吓你個護照。
	Mh'gōi béi ngóh tái-háh néih go wuhjiu.
You're in the wrong seat.	你坐錯位喇
	Néih chóh-cho wái* la.
You have made a mistake.	你搞錯咗喇
	Néih gáau-cho-jó le.
This seat is reserved.	呢個位有人訂咗喇
	Nī go wái* yáuh yàhn dehng-jó la.
You have to pay extra.	你需要俾多啲錢。
	Néih sēuiyiu béi dō-dī chín*.

The ... has been delayed by ... minutes.	... 將會晚點 ... 分鐘 ... jēung wúih máahndím ... fānjūng.

6.3 Tickets

Where can I...?	我去邊度 ... 呀? Ngóh heui bīndouh ... a?
– buy a ticket?	買飛 máaih-fēi
– reserve a seat?	訂位 dehng-wái*
– reserve a flight?	訂機票 dehng-gēipiu
Could I have...for...please?	唔該俾...張去嘅車飛。 M̀h'gōi béi ... jēung heui ... ge chēfēi.
A single to...please	唔該俾一張單程票去... M̀h'gōi béi yāt jēung dāanchìhng-piu heui ...
A return ticket, please	唔該俾一張來回票去... M̀h'gōi, béi yāt jēung lòihwùih-piu heui ...
first class	頭等艙。 tàuhdáng-chōng
second class	商務艙。 sēungmouh-chōng
economy class	經濟艙。 gīngjai-chōng
I'd like to reserve a seat/berth/cabin	我想訂個座位／臥舖／車廂。 Ngóh séung dehng go johwái*/ngohpōu/chēsēung.
I'd like to reserve a top/bottom berth in the sleeping car	我想訂個上舖／下舖。 Ngóh séung dehng go seuhngpou/hahpōu.
Where's the information desk?	詢問處喺邊度呀? Sēunmahn-chyu hái bīndouh a?

6.4 Information

Where can I find a schedule?	邊度有時間表呀? Bīndouh yáuh sìhgaan-bíu a?
Where's the...desk?	...台喺／響邊度呀? ... tòih hái/héung bīndouh a?
Do you have a city map with the bus/the subway routes on it?	有冇巴士／地鐵路線圖呀? Yáuhmóuh bāsí/deihtit louhsin-tòuh a?
Do you have a schedule?	有冇時間表呀? Yáuh-móuh sìhgaan-bíu a?
Will I get my money back?	可唔可以攞番錢呀? Hó-m̀h-hóyíh ló-fāan chín* a?
I'd like to confirm/cancel/change my reservation for/trip to...	我想確認／取消／改變我預定去...嘅旅程。 Ngóh séung kokyihng/chéuisīu/góibin ngóh yuhdihng heui ... ge léuihchìhng.

I'd like to go to...	我想去 … Ngóh séung heui ...
What is the quickest way to get there?	去 … 最快嘅路程係邊條呀? Heui ... jeuifaai ge louhchìhng haih bīn tìuh a?
How much is a single/return to...?	去 … 嘅單程 / 來回係幾多錢呀? Heui ... ge dāanchìhng/lòihwùih haih géidō chín* a?
Do I have to pay extra?	駛唔駛俾多啲錢呀? Sái-m̀h-sái béi dō-dī chín* a?
How much luggage am I allowed?	可以帶幾多行李呀? Hóyíh daai géidō hàhngléih a?
Is this a direct train?	係唔係直通車呀? Haih-m̀h-haih jihktūng-chē a?
Do I have to change?	駛唔駛轉巴士 / 火車 / 飛機呀? Sái-m̀h-sái jyun bāsí/fóchē/fēigēi a?
Where?	喺 / 響邊度轉巴士 / 火車 / 飛機呀? Hái/héung bīndouh jyun bāsí/fóchē/fēigēi a?
Does the plane stop anywhere?	飛機中途停留啲乜嘢地方呀? Fēigēi jūngtòuh tìhnglàuh dī mātyéh deihfōng a?
Will there be any stopovers?	中途要停留嗎? Jūngtòuh yiu tìhnglàuh ma?
Does the boat stop at any other ports on the way?	(客) 船中途要停其他碼頭嗎? (Haak)syùhn jūngtòuh yiu tìhng kèihtā máhtàuh ma?
Does the train/bus stop at...?	火車 / 巴士喺 / 響 … 停嗎? Fóchē/bāsí hái/héung ... tìhng ma?
Where do I get off?	喺 / 響邊度落 (車 / 船) ? Hái/héng bīndouh lohk-chē/syùhn?
Is there a connection to...?	有冇車接住去 … ? Yáuh-móuh chē jip-jyuh heui ...?
How long do I have to wait?	要等幾耐呀? Yiu dáng géi noih a?
When does the bus/train leave?	呢班巴士 / 火車幾點開車呀? Nī bāan bāsí/fóchē géidím hōi-chē a? /
When does the boat leave?	呢班船幾點開呀? Nī bāan syùhn géidím hōi a?
When does the plane leave?	呢班飛機幾點起飛呀? Nī bāan fēigēi géidím héifēi a?
What time does the first/last (bus/train) leave?	頭班 / 尾班車幾點開呀? Tàuh bāan / méih bāan chē géidím hōi a?
What time does the first/last boat leave?	頭班 / 尾班船幾點開呀? Tàuh bāan / méih bāan syùhn géidím hōi a?
What time does the first/last plane leave?	頭班 / 尾班飛機幾時開呀? Tàuh bāan / méih bāan fēigēi géidím hōi a?
What time does the next (bus/train) leave?	下一班巴士 / 火車幾點開呀? Hah yāt bāan chē/fóchē géidím hōi a?
What time does the next boat leave?	下一班船幾點開呀? Hah yāt bāan syùhn géidím hōi a?
What time does the next plane leave?	下一班飛機幾點飛呀? Hah yāt bāan fēigēi géidím fēi a?

Public transportation

How long does...take?	... 需要幾長時間呀？
	... sēuiyiu géi chèuhng sìhgaan a?
What time does... arrive in...?	... 幾時到 ... ？
	... géidím dou ... ?
Where does the bus/train to...leave from?	去 ... 嘅巴士／火車幾點開車呀？
	Heui ... ge bāsí/fóchē géidím hōi-chē a?
Where does the boat to...leave from?	去 ... 嘅船幾點開呀？
	Heui ... ge syùhn géidím hōi a?
Where does the plane to...leave from?	去 ... 嘅飛機幾點起飛呀？
	Heui ... ge fēigēi géidím héifēi a?
Is this the train/bus to...?	呢班火車／巴士 ... 嗎？
	Nī bāan fóchē/bāsí heui ... ma?

6.5 Airplanes

On arrival at the Hongkong International (Chek Lap Kok) Airport (Gwokjai Gēichèuhng 國際機場), you will find the following signs:

登機處	國內航班	出境
check-in	domestic flights	departures
國際	入境	
international	arrivals	

6.6 Long-distance trains

As an extension to its domestic passenger service between Hung Hom (Hùhngham 紅磡) and the boundary at Lo Wu (Lòhwùh 羅湖), the Kowloon-Canton Railway provides inter-city train services to and from Shenzhen, Guangzhou, Shanghai and Beijing. Two classes of tickets are available: soft and hard. For soft class, there are 8 berths per cabin with 4 passengers per berth. For hard class, 66 seats are available. You will need a valid travel document for Mainland China.

The train to ... is now arriving at platform...	開往 ... 嘅列車，而家到達 ... 號月臺。
	Hōiwóhng ... ge liht chē, yìhgā doudaaht ... houh yuhttòih.
The train from ... is now arriving at platform...	由 ... 開出嘅列車，而家到達 ... 號月臺。
	Yàuh ... hōi-chēut ge lihtchē, yìhgā doudaaht ... houh yuhttòih.
The train to ... will leave from platform...	開往 ... 嘅列車，而家喺 ... 號月臺離站。
	Hōi wóhng ... ge lihtchē, yìhgā hái ...houh yuhttòih lèih-jaahm.
Today the [time] train to ... will leave from platform...	今日...點開往 ... 嘅列車，而家喺 ... 號月臺離站。
	Gāmyaht ... dím hōi wóhng ... ge lihtchē, yìhgā hái ...houh yuhttòih lèih-jaahm.
Where does this train go to?	呢班火車去邊度呀？
	Nī bāan fóchē heui bīndouh a?
Please don't stand too close to the train doors	請勿靠近車門。
	Chíng maht kaaugahn chēmùhn.
Mind the gap between the train and the platform	請小心月臺間之空隙。
	Chíng síusām yuhttòih gāan jī hūngkwīk.

6

Public transportation

The next station is...	下個站係... Hah go jaahm haih ...
Please let passengers get off the train first.	請先讓乘客落車。 Chíng sīn yeuhng sìhnghaak lohk-chē.
Please use the left-hand side door to alight from the train	請喺／響左邊車門落車。 Chíng hái/héung jóbīn chēmùhn lohk-chē.
Please go to the opposite platform to change trains to ...	請到對面月臺轉車。 Chíng dou deuimihn yuhttòih jyun-chē.
Could you let me know when we get to...?	請問，去...站應該幾時落車？ Chíngmahn, heui ... yīnggōi géisìh lohk-chē?
Could you stop at the next stop, please?	唔該，我下個站落車。 M̀h'gōi, ngóh hah go jaahm lohk-chē.
Where are we?	我哋而家喺／響邊度呀？ Ngóhdeih yìhgā hái/héung bīndouh a?
Can I get off the train for a while?	我可唔可以落火車一陣呀？ Ngóh hó-m̀h-hóyíh lohk fóchē yātjahn a?
Do I have to get off here?	我係唔係要喺呢度落車呀？ Ngóh haih-m̀h-haih yiu hái nīdouh lohk-chē a?

6.7 Taxis

Taxis provide a reasonably priced and efficient means of getting about in Hong Kong. You can pick up your taxi at hotels or hail them on the street. You may want to ask your driver (sīgēi 司機) to wait for you while you are on sightseeing trips or finishing your business as waiting time is not expensive. Most taxi drivers speak English.

It is not common to rent your own car to drive around Hong Kong. If you choose to do so, there are three companies to choose from — Avis, Trinity and DCH.

出租 for hire	有人 occupied	的士站 taxi stand

Taxi!	的士 dīksí!
Could you get me a taxi, please?	唔該幫我叫一架的士。 M̀h'gōi bōng ngóh giu yāt ga dīksí.
Where can I find a taxi around here?	邊度有的士叫呀？ Bīndouh yáuh dīksí giu a?
Could you take me to..., please?	唔該揸我去 ... M̀h'goi jā ngóh heui ...
Could you take me to this address, please	唔該揸我去呢個地址。 M̀h'goi jā ngóh heui nī go deihjí.
– to the...hotel, please	唔該揸我去 ... 酒店。 M̀h'goi jā ngóh heui ... jáudim.
– to the town/city center, please	唔該揸我去市區。 M̀h'goi jā ngóh heui síhkēui.
– to the station, please	唔該揸我去 ... 火車站。 M̀h'goi jā ngóh heui ... fóchē-jaahm.

– to the airport, please	唔該揸我去 ... 機場。 Mh'goi jā ngóh heui ... gēichèuhng.
How much is the trip to...?	去 ... 幾多錢? Heui ... géidō chín*?
How far is it to...?	呢度離 ... 有幾遠? Nīdouh lèih ... yáuh géi yúhn?
Could you turn on the meter, please (driver)?	司機,唔該你打表。 Sīgēi ... Mh'gōi néih dá-bīu.
I'm in a hurry	我趕時間。 Ngóh gón sìhgaan.
Could you speed up/ slow down a little?	可以揸快啲 / 慢啲嗎? Hóyíh jā faai-dī/maahn-dī ma?
Could you take a different route?	可以行第二條路嗎? Hóyíh hàahng daihyih tìuh louh ma?
I'd like to get out here, please	我喺 / 響呢度落車。 Ngóh hái/héung nīdouh lohk-chē.
I'd like to rent a Japanese car.	我想租一架日本車。 Ngóh séung jōu yāt ga Yahtbún-chē.
How much does it cost to hire ... ?	租 ... 要幾多錢? Jōu ... yiu géidō chín*?
– per day	一日 yāt yaht
– two days	兩日 léuhng yaht
– per kilometer	每公里 múih gūngléih
How many kilometers per day do I get for the basic fee?	一日嘅收費可以行幾多公里呀? Yāt yaht ge sāufai hóyíh hàhng géidō gungléih a?
Does the price include gas?	價錢包唔包括電油? Gachìhn bāau-mh-bāaukut dihnyàuh?
Go	行得 Hàahng-dāk
You have to go...here	喺 / 響呢度 ... 去 Hái/héung nīdouh ... heui.
Go straight ahead	一直去。 Yātjihk heui.
Go till end of road	行到盡頭。 hàahng-dou jeuhntàuh
Turn left	轉左 jyun jó.
Turn right	轉右 jyun yauh.
This is it/We're here	呢度就係。 / 到喇。 / Nīdouh jauh haih. / Dou la. /
Could you wait a minute for me, please?	可以等我一陣嗎? Hóyíh dáng ngóh yātjahn ma?
How much do I owe you?	幾多錢呀? Géidō chín* a'?

Public transportation

7

Overnight accommodation

7.1 General 69

7.2 Booking 70

7.3 Checking the room 71

7.4 Requests 72

7.5 Complaints 74

7.6 Departure 75

7 Overnight accommodation

7.1 General

● **In Hong Kong,** there is no star classification in hotels. However, at the top end, hotel (jáudim 酒店) accommodation comes with swimming pools, sauna, restaurants. For back-packers, there are youth hostels offered by the YMCA and the YWCA (nàahm/néuih'chīngnìhn-wúi* 男／女青年會) with shared bunker-type accommodation, common bathroom and toilet facilities. They are both located in Mongkok (Wohnggok 旺角). There are two more with similar grading: they are New King Hostel in Yau Ma Tei (Yàuhmàhdéi* 油麻地) and Nathan Hostel in Jordan (jódēun 佐敦), all four are located in Kowloon (Gáulùhng 九龍).

I'm looking for a cheap/good hotel.	我要搵間平／好嘅酒店。 Ngóh yiu wán gāan pèhng/hóu ge jáudim.
I'm looking for a nearby hotel.	我要搵一間近嘅酒店。 Ngóh yiu wán yāt gāan káhn ge jáudim.
Do you give discounts for students?	留學生有冇優待？ Làuhhohk-sāang yáuh-móuh yāudoih?
I'm not sure how long I'm staying.	我唔知會住幾耐。 Ngóh m̀h'jī wúih jyuh géi noih.
Do you have any rooms?	有冇空房？ Yáuh-móuh hūngfóng*?
Do you have air-conditioning/heating in the room?	房入邊有冇空調／暖氣？ Fóng* yahpbihn yáh-móuh hūngtiùh/nyúhnhei?
Do you have room service?	有冇送酒菜都到房間嘅服務？ Yáuh-móuh sung jáuchoi dou fòhnggāan ge fuhkmouh?
Where's the emergency exit/fire escape?	緊急／消防通道喺／響邊度呀？ Gán'gāp/sīufòhng tūngdouh hái/héung bīndouh a?
The key to room..., please	唔該俾 … 號房鎖匙我。 M̀h'gōi béi ... houh fóng* ge sósìh ngóh.
Could you put this in the safe, please?	唔該放喺／響夾萬入邊。 M̀h'gōi fong hái/héung gaapmaahn yahpbihn.
Could you wake me at...tomorrow?	唔該聽日 … 點叫醒我。 M̀h'gōi tīngyaht ...dím giuséng ngóh.
Could I have an extra blanket?	唔該俾多一張氈我。 M̀h'gōi béi do yāt jēung jīn ngóh.
What time does the gate/door open/close?	幾點開門／閂門？ Géidím hōi-mùhn / sāan-mùhn?
Could you get me a taxi, please?	唔該幫我叫架的士。 M̀h'gōi bōng ngóh giu ga dīksí.
Could you find a babysitter for me?	可唔可以幫我搵個保姆？ Hó-m̀h-hóyíh bōng ngóh wán go bóumóuh?
Is there any mail for me?	我有冇信呀？ Ngóh yáuh-móuh seun a?

唔該你填呢張表格。	Fill out this form, please
唔該俾我睇吓你個護照。	Could I see your passport?
你需要俾按金。	I'll need a deposit

7.2 Booking

My name is...	我個名叫做 ...
	Ngóh go méng* giujouh ...
I've made a reservation.	我已經訂咗房。
	Ngóh yíhgīng dehng-jó fóng*.
I wrote to you last month.	我上個月寫過信俾你哋。
	Ngóh seuhng go yuht sé-gwo seun béi néihdeih.
Here's the confirmation.	呢張係確認單。
	Nī jēung haih kokyihng-dāan.
How much is it per night/week?	呢間房住一晚 / 一個星期幾多錢?
	Nī gāan fóng* jyuh yāt máahn / yāt go sīngkèih géidō chín*?
We'll be staying for ...nights/weeks.	我哋打算住 ... 日 / (個) 星期
	Ngóhdeih dásyun jyuh ... yaht / (go) sīngkèih.
I'd like a single/double room.	我要一間單人房 / 雙人房。
	Ngóh yiu yāt gāan dāanyàhn-fóng*/sēungyàhn-fóng*.
per person/per room	一個人 / 一間房
	yāt go yàhn / yāt gāan fóng*
I'd like a room with ...	我要一間有 ... 嘅房。
	Ngóh yiu yāt gāan yáuh ... ge fóng*.
twin beds	兩張單人床
	léuhng jēung dāanyàhn-chòhng
a double bed	一張單人床
	yāt jēung dāanyàhn-chòhng
a bath tub	浴缸
	yuhkgōng
a shower	花洒
	fāsá
a balcony	陽臺
	yèuhngtòih
a suite	一間套房
	yāt gāan toufóng*
Could we have two adjoining rooms?	有冇兩間房喺一齊嘅套房?
	Yáuh-móuh léuhng gāan fóng* hái yātchàih ge toufóng*?
Does that include breakfast?	房價係唔係包括早餐呀?
	Fòhngga haih-m̀h-haih bāaukut jóuchāan a?
We'd like a room ...	我哋要一間 ... 房。
	Ngóhdeih yiu yāt gāan ... fóng*.
facing the front	對正前面嘅
	deuijing chìhnmihn ge

Overnight accommodation

7

at the back	對正後面嘅 deuijing hauhmihn ge
with street/river/sea view	對正大街／河／海嘅 deuijing daaihgāai/hòh/hói ge
Is there...in the room?	房入邊有冇...? Fóng* yahpbihn yáuh-móuh ... ?
air conditioning	空調 hūngtiuh
heating	暖氣 nyúnhei
TV	電視 dihnsih
refrigerator	雪櫃 syut'gwaih
hot water	熱水 yihtséui
electric jug	電水壺 dihnséui-wú*

7.3 Checking the room

Could I see the room?	我可以睇吓間房嗎? Ngóh hóyíh tái-háh gāan fóng* ma?
We don't like this one	我唔鐘意呢間。 Ngóh m̀h'jūngyi nī gaan.
Do you have another room?	仲有冇第啲嘅房呀? Juhng yáuh-móuh daihdī ge fóng* a?
Do you have a larger room?	有冇大啲嘅房呀? Yáuh-móuh daaih-dī ge fóng* a?
Do you have a less expensive room?	有冇平啲嘅房呀? Yáuh-móuh pèhng-dī ge fóng* a?
We prefer a quiet room	我哋鐘意靜啲嘅房。 Ngóhdeih jūngyi jihng-dī ge fóng*.
No, they are all occupied.	冇喇, 都住滿喇。 Móuh la, dōu jyuh-múhn la.
This room is too ...	呢間房太...喇。 Nī gāan fóng* taai ... la.
hot/cold	熱／凍 yiht/dung
dark/small	黑／細 hāk/sai

唔該跟我嚟吖。	This way please
你（哋）間房喺... 樓 ...號房。	Your room is on the...floor, number...
廁所同冲涼房喺／響同一層。	The toilet and shower are on the same floor.
廁所同冲涼房喺埋一間房。	The toilet and shower are in the room

noisy	嘈
	chòh
I'll take this room	我就要呢間房。
	Ngóh jauh yiu nī gāan fóng*.
Could you put in a cot?	可唔可以加一張嬰兒床呀?
	Hó-mh-hóyíh gā yāt jēung yīngyìh-chòhng a?
What time's breakfast?	幾點食早餐呀?
	Géidím sihk-jóuchāan a?
Where's the dining room?	餐廳喺 / 響邊度呀?
	Chāantēng hái/héung bīndouh a?
Can I have breakfast in my room?	可以喺 / 響房入邊食早餐嗎?
	Hóyíh hái/héung fóng* yahpbihn sihk jóuchāan ma?
How much is the room per night?	呢間房幾錢一晚呀?
	Nī gāan fóng* géi chín* yāt máahn a?
Does this include ...?	包唔包...?
	Bāau-mh-bāau ...?
breakfast	早餐
	jóuchāan
three meals	三餐
	sāamchāan
service	服務費
	fuhkmouh-fai

7.4 Requests

Overnight accommodation

I need a two-prong plug.	我需要一個雙插頭。
	Ngóh sēuiyiu yāt go sēung chaaptàuh.
I need a three-prong plug.	我需要一個三插頭。
	Ngóh sēuiyiu yāt go sāam chaaptàuh.
I need this kind of plug.	我需要一個瞰樣嘅插頭。
	Ngóh sēuiyiu yāt go gámyéung* ge chaaptàuh.
Where's the plug for the razor?	剃鬚嘅插頭喺 / 響邊度呀?
	Tai-sōu ge chaaptàuh hái/héung bīndouh a?
What's the voltage?	呢度嘅電壓係幾多伏?
	Nīdouh ge dihn'ngaat haih géidō fuhk?
May I have ...?	可唔可以俾我...?
	Hó-mh-hóyíh béi ngóh ... ?
(more) hangers	...個衣架
	... go yīgá*
a needle and some thread	一枝針同埋一啲線
	yāt jī jāam tùhngmàaih yātdī sin.
(more) blankets	... 多張氈
	... dō jēung jīn
(another) pillow	(多一個) 枕頭
	(dō yāt go) jámtàuh
an envelope	(一個) 信封
	(yāt go) seunfūng
some stationery	信紙
	seunjí

72

soap	番硯
	fāan'gáan
shampoo	洗頭水
	sáitàuh-séui
bath lotion	沐浴液
	muhkyuhk-yihk
bath towel	浴巾
	yuhkgān
cold drinking water	凍滾水
	dung gwánséui
hot drinking water	滾水
	gwánséui
Can you repair this ... ?	可唔可以幫我修理呢 (個)...
	Hó-m̀h-hóyíh bōng ngóh sāuléih nī (go) ...
camera	影相機
	yíngséung-gēi
video camera	攝錄機
	sipluhk-gēi
suitcase	皮夾
	pèihgīp
The room needs to be cleaned.	唔該打掃一吓房間。
	M̀h'gōi dásou-yātháh fòhnggāan.
Please change the sheets/towels.	唔該換一吓床單／毛巾
	M̀h'gōi wuhn-yātháh chòhngdāan/mòuhgān.
Please send my breakfast/lunch/dinner to my room	唔該將早餐／午餐／晚餐送到我間房嚟。
	M̀h'gōi jēung jóuchāan/ńghchāan/máahnchāan sung dou ngóh gāan fóng* làih.
I'd like these clothes ...	唔該將呢啲衣服 ...
	Mhgōi jēung nīdī yīfuhk ...
washed	洗乾淨
	sái-gōnjehng
ironed	熨直
	tong-jihk
dry-cleaned	乾洗
	gōnsái
I'm leaving tonight. Can I put my laundry in?	我今晚就走，仲可以洗衣服嗎？
	Ngóh gāmmáahn jauh jáu, juhng hóyíh sái yīfuhk ma?
Is my laundry ready?	我啲衣服洗好未呀？
	Ngóh dī yīfuhk sái-hóu meih a?
I need it at	我 ... 要。
	Ngóh ... yiu.
today	今日
	gāmyaht
tonight	今晚
	gāmmáahn
tomorrow	聽日
	tīngyaht
I want it as soon as possible.	越快越好。
	Yuht faai yuht hóu.

Can you sew on this button?	唔該幫我釘番呢粒鈕。
	Mh'gōi bōng ngóh dēng-fāan nī lāp náu.
This isn't mine.	呢件（衫）唔係我嘅。
	Nī gihn (sāam) mh'haih ngóh ge.
There is one piece missing.	我少咗一件。
	Ngóh síu-jó yāt gihn.
Is my laundry ready?	我啲衫洗好未呀？
	Ngóh dī sāam sái-hóu meih a?
I'm leaving soon, but my laundry is not back yet.	我就快要走喇，但係洗咗嗰啲衫仲未返嚟喎。
	Ngóh jauh faai yiu jáu la, daahnhaih sái-jó gódī sāam juhng meih fāan-làih woh.

7.5 Complaints

We can't sleep for the noise	太嘈喇，我哋瞓唔着。
	Taai chòuh la, ngóhdeih fan-mh'jeuhk.
Could you turn the radio/hi-fi/TV down, please?	唔該將收音機／音響／電視較低一啲。
	Mh'gōi jēung sāuyām-gēi/yāmhéung/dihnsih gaau-dāi yāt-dī.
We're out of toilet paper	廁紙用完喇。
	Chíjí yuhng-yùhn la.
There aren't any.../ there's not enough...	冇...喇／唔夠...
	Móuh ... la / Mh'gau ...
The bed linen's dirty	床單係污糟嘅。
	Chòhngdāan haih wūjōu ge.
The room hasn't been cleaned	（間）房冇執過。
	(Gāan) fóng* móuh jāp-gwo.
The heating isn't working	暖氣有問題，都唔熱嘅。
	Nyúhnhei yáuh mahntàih, dōu mh'yiht gé.
There's no (hot) water/electricity	冇熱水／電喇。
	Móuh yihtséui/dihn la.
...doesn't work/is broken	...唔郁／壞咗。
	... mh'yūk / waaih-jó
The toilet is blocked.	廁所塞咗。
	Chisó sāk-jó.
The sink is blocked.	洗碗盤塞咗。
	Sáiwún-pùhn sāk-jó
The tap is dripping.	水喉漏水。
	Séuihàuh lauhséui
The bulb is burnt out.	燈膽燒咗。
	dāngdáam sīu-jó.
The blind is broken.	百葉簾拉唔郁。
	Baakyihp-lím* lāai-mh'yūk
Could you have that seen to?	唔該你搵人整吓
	Mh'gōi néih wán yàhn jíng-háh
Could I have another room?	我可唔可以要第二間房呀？
	Ngóh hó-mh'hóyíh yiu daihyih gāan fóng* a?
The bed creaks terribly	張床好大聲。
	Jēung chòhng hóu daaihsēng.
The bed sags	張床凹咗落去。
	Jēung chòhng lāp-jó lohk-heui.

It's too noisy _____	呢度太嘈喇。
	Nīdouh taai chòh la.
This place is full of _____ mosquitos	呢度周圍都有蚊。
	Nīdouh jāuwàih dōu yáuh mān.
– cockroaches _____	甲由。
	gaahtjáat

7.6 Departure

See also 8.2 Settling the bill

I'm leaving (the hotel) _____ tomorrow	我聽日走。
	Ngóh tīngyaht jáu.
Where can I pay my bill, _____ please?	請問，去邊度找數／埋單？
	Chíngmahn, heui bīndouh jáau-sou/màaih-dāan?
My room number is ... _____	我間房嘅號碼係 ...
	Ngóh gāan fóng* ge houhmáh haih ...
What time should we _____ check out?	我應該幾時辦離店手續？
	Ngóh yīnggōi géisìh baahn lèih-dim sáujuhk?
I'm leaving early _____ tomorrow. Please have my bill ready.	我聽日一早就要走，唔該你預先準備好帳單。
	Ngóh tīngyaht yāt jóu jauh yiu jáu, m̀h'gōi néih yuhsīn jéunbeih-hóu jeungdāan.
Could I have my deposit _____ back, please?	唔該俾番訂金我。
	M̀h'gōi béi-fāan dehnggām ngóh.
I must leave at once. _____	我而家就要走。
	Ngóh yìhgā jauh yiu jáu.
Is this my bill? _____	呢張係唔係我嘅帳單呀？
	Nī jēung haih-m̀h-haih ngóh ge jeungdāan a?
Is everything included? _____	係唔係所有嘅費用都包括喺／響入邊呀？
	Haih-m̀h haih sóyáuh ge faiyuhng dōu baaukut hái yahpbihn a?
Do you accept credit _____ cards?	你哋收唔收信用卡呀？
	Néihdeih sāu-m̀h-sāu seunyuhng-kāat a?
(I reckon) you've made _____ a mistake in the bill.	呢張單係唔係計錯呀？
	Nī jēung dāan haih-m̀h-haih gai-cho a?
Could you forward my _____ mail to this address?	唔該將我啲信轉寄到呢個地址。
	M̀h'gōi jēung ngóh dī seun jyúngei-dou nī go deihjí.
Could we leave our _____ luggage here until we leave?	可唔可以存啲行李喺度，我一陣返嚟攞？
	Hó-m̀h-hóyíh chyùhn dī hàhnglèih hái douh, ngóh yātjahn fāanlàih ló?
Thanks for your hospitality	多謝你哋嘅熱情招待。
	Dōjeh néihdeih ge yihtchìhng jīudoih.
We enjoyed it, thank you. _____	我哋住得好滿意，多謝。
	Ngóhdeih jyuh-dāk hóu múhnyi, dōjeh.

Money matters

8.1 **B**anks 77

8.2 **S**ettling the bill 78

M̲oney matters

● **In general**, banks are open to the public Monday to Friday from 9:00 a.m. to 4:30 p.m. , Saturday from 9:00 a.m. to 1:00 p.m., but it is always possible to exchange money in hotels or other tourist centers. Your passport is usually required when exchanging currency.

8 .1 Banks

Where can I change foreign currency?	去邊度可以換錢呀？ Heui bīndouh hóyíh wuhn-chín* a?
Where can I cash this traveler's check?	去邊度可以換旅行支票呀？ Heui bīndouh hóyíh wuhn léuihhàhng jīpiu a?
Can I cash this...here?	可唔可以係 / 響呢度換...呀？ Hó-m̀h-hóyíh hái/héung nīdouh wuhn .... a?
What's today's exchange rate for ...?	今日兌換 ... 嘅兌換率係幾多呀？ Gāmyaht deuiwuhn ... ge deuiwuhn-léut* haih géidō a ?
– US dollars	美金 Meihgām
– English pounds	英鎊 Yīngbóng*
– Japanese Yen	日元 Yahtyùhn
– Canadian dollars	加幣 Gābaih
– Australian dollars	澳幣 Ngoubaih
– Hong Kong dollars	港幣 Góngbaih
Can I withdraw money on my credit card here?	呢度可唔可以用信用卡攞錢呀？ Nīdouh hó-m̀h-hóyíh yuhng seunyuhng-kāat ló-chín* a?
What's the maximum amount?	一次最多可以攞幾多錢？ Yāt chi jeuidō hóyíh ló géidō chín*?
What's the minimum amount?	一次最少要攞幾多錢？ Yāt chi jeuisíu yiu ló géidō chín*?
Can I take out less than that?	我唔攞咁多得唔得呀？ Ngóh m̀h'ló gam dō dak-m̀h-dāk a?
I had some money cabled here	有人電匯咗啲錢俾我。 Yáuh yàhn dihnwuih-jó dī chín* béi ngóh.
Has it arrived yet?	嚟咗未呀？ Làih-jó meih a?
I'm expecting some money from ...	我等緊喺 / 響...匯嚟嚟嗰啲錢。 Ngóh dáng-gán hái/héung ... wuih-gán-làih gó dī chín*.
These are the details of my bank in the US	呢啲係我喺 / 響美國嗰間銀行嘅資料。 Nīdī haih ngóh hái/héung Méihgwok gó gāan ngàhnhòhng ge jīlíu*.

77

This is the number of my bank account	呢個係我嘅銀行賬戶號碼。 Nī go haih ngóh ge ngàhnhòhng jeung'wuh houhmáh.
Could you write it down for me?	你可唔可以寫低俾我? Néih hó-m̀h-hóyíh sé-dāi béi ngóh?
I'd like to change some money	我想換錢。 Ngóh séung wuhn-chín*.
– pounds into...	英鎊換 ... 。 Yīngbohng wuhn ...
– dollars into...	美金換 ... 。 Méihgām wuhn ...
What's the exchange rate?	兌換率係幾多? Deuiwuhn-léut* haih géidō?
Could you give me some small change with it?	唔該俾啲散紙我。 M̀h'gōi béi dī sáanjí ngóh.
This is not right	呢度唔啱數。 Nīdouh m̀h'ngāamsou.

唔該喺 / 響呢度簽名。	Sign here, please
唔該你填呢張表格。	Fill this out, please
唔該俾我睇吓你嘅護照。	Could I see your passport, please?
唔該俾我睇吓你嘅身份証。	Could I see your identity card, please?
唔該俾我睇吓你嘅信用咭。	Could I see your credit card, please?

8.2 Settling the bill

Could you put it on my bill?	唔該入埋我張單嗰度。 M̀h'gōi yahp-màaih ngóh jēung dāan gódouh.
Is everything included?	係唔係所有嘢都包括咗? Haih-m̀h-haih sóyáuh yéh dōu bāaukut-jó?
Is the tip included?	係唔係已經包括咗貼士? Haih-m̀h-haih yíhgīng bāaukut-jó tīpsí*?
Can I pay by...?	我可以用 ... 俾錢嗎? Ngóh hóyíh yuhng ... béi-chín* ma?
Can I pay by credit card?	我可以用信用卡俾錢嗎? Ngóh hóyíh yuhng seunyuhng-kāat béi-chín* ma?
Can I pay by traveler's check?	我可以用旅行支票俾錢嗎? Ngóh hóyíh yuhng léuihhàhng jīpiu béi-chín* ma?
Can I pay with foreign currency?	我可以用外幣俾錢嗎? Ngóh hóyíh yuhng ngoihbaih béi-chín* ma?
You've given me too much change	你找多咗錢俾我喇。 Néih jáau-dō-jó chín* béi ngóh la.
You haven't given me enough change	你找唔夠錢俾我。 Néih jáau-m̀h'gau chín* béi ngóh.

Could you check this _____ again, please?	唔該你再數一下。 M̀h'gōi néih joi sóu yāt-háh.
Could I have a receipt, _____ please?	唔該俾張收據我。 M̀h'gōi béi jēung sāugeui ngóh.
I don't have enough _____ money on me	我帶唔夠錢。 Ngóh daaih-m̀h'gau chín*.
This is for you _____	呢啲係俾你嘅貼士。 Nīdī haih béi néih ge tīpsí*.
Keep the change _____	唔駛找。 M̀h'sái jáau.

(對唔住)，我哋唔收信用卡／ 旅行支票／外幣。	We don't accept credit cards/traveler's checks/ foreign currency

Money matters 8

Mail and telephone

9.1 Mail   81

9.2 Telephone   82

Mail and telephone

9.1 Mail

See 8 Money matters

● **Post offices** are open Monday to Friday from 9:00 a.m. to 5:00 p.m. and half day on Saturday from 9:00 a.m. to 12:00 noon. The cost of sending a letter, either by surface or air mail, depends on its weight.

郵票 stamps	電匯 /（郵政 / 銀行） 匯票 money orders	包裹 parcels
電報 telegrams		

Where is...?	... 喺 / 響邊度? ... hái/héung bīndouh?
– the nearest post office?	最近嘅郵局 jeuikáhn ge yàuhgúk*
– the main post office	郵政總局 yàuhjing júnggúk*
– the nearest mail box?	... 最近嘅信箱? jeuikáhn ge seunsēung
Which counter should I go to...?	... 去邊個櫃檯? ... heui bīn go gwaihtói*?
Which counter should I go to to send a fax?	發傳真去邊個櫃檯? Faat-chyùhnjān heui bīn go gwaihtói*?
Which counter should I go to to wire a money order?	電匯去邊個櫃檯? Dihnwuih heui bīn go gwaihtói*?
Which counter should I go to for general delivery?	攞郵件去邊個櫃檯? Ló yàuhgín* heui bīn go gwaihtói*?
Is there any mail for me?	有冇我嘅信? Yáuh-móuh ngóh ge seun?
My name"s...	我叫做 ... Ngóh giujouh ....

Stamps

What's the postage for a letter/postcard to...?	寄信 / 明信片到 ... 嘅郵費係幾多錢? Gei seun/mìhngseun-pín* dou ... ge yàuhfai haih géidō chín*?
Are there enough stamps on it?	郵票夠唔夠? Yàuhpiu gauh-m̀h-gauh?
I'd like [quantity] [value] stamps	我要［... 張］... 嘅郵票。 Ngóh yiu [... jēung] ... ge yàuhpiu.
I'd like to send this...	我想寄 ... Ngóh séung gei ...
– express	快郵 faaiyàuh
– by air mail	航空 hòhnghūng

– by registered mail	挂號 gwahouh
– by surface mail	海運 hóiwahn

Telegram / fax

I'd like to send a telegram to...	我想發電報去 ... Ngóh séung faat dihnbou heui ...
How much is that per word?	幾多錢一個字 Géidō chín* yāt go jih?
This is the text I want to send	呢張係我要發嘅稿。 Nī jēung haih ngóh yiu faat ge góu.
Shall I fill out the form myself?	係唔係我自己填呢張表格呀? Haih-m̀h-haih ngóh jihgéi tìhn nī jēung bíugaak a?
Can I make photocopies/ send a fax here?	呢度可唔可以複印 / 發傳真呀? Nīdouh hó-m̀h-hóyíh fūkyan/faat-chyùhnjān a?
How much is it per page?	幾多錢一頁呀? Géidō chín* yāt yihp a?

9.2 Telephone

Direct international calls can easily be made from public telephones using either coins or phone cards. The latter is most commonly used and they are available from convenient shops such as 7-eleven and companies selling telephones and mobile networks. Phone cards have a value of HK$100. Dial 00 to get out of Hong Kong, then the relevant country code (USA 1), city code and number. It depends very much on which phone card company you are using. An example is 001/007/0060/1666, then the relevant country code, city code and number. To find a telephone number in Hong Kong, ring 1081. All operators speak English for English enquiries.

Is there a phone booth around here?	附近有冇公眾電話呀? Fuhgahn yáuh-móuh gūngjung dihnwá* a?
May I use your phone, please?	我可以借用你嘅電話嗎? Ngóh hóyíh jeyuhng néih ge dihnwá* ma?
Do you have a (city/region) phone directory?	有冇電話簿呀? Yáuh-móuh dihnwá*bóu a?
Where can I get a phone card?	邊度可以買到電話咭呀? Bīndouh hóyíh máaih-dóu dihnwá*-kāat a?
Could you give me...?	唔該幫我查一下... M̀h'gōi bōng ngóh chàh-yātháh ...
– the number of room...?	... 號房嘅電話號碼 ... houh fóng* ge dihnwá* houhmáh.
– the number for international directory assistance?	國際電話服務處嘅號碼 gwokjai dihnwá* fuhkmouh-chyu ge houhmáh.
– the international access code?	國際長途電話嘅號碼 gwokjai chèuhngtòuh dihnwá* ge houhmáh.
– the country code?	國家代號 ... gwokgā doihhouh

– the area code for...?	... 嘅地區號
	... ge deihkēui houh
Do I need to dial "0" first (before dialing out from the hotel)?	打出去要撥 "零" 嗎?
	Dá-chéut-heui yiu buht lìhng" ma?
Yes, calling for outside connections needs to dial "0" first.	要, 打外線要先撥"零"。
	Yiu, dá-ngoihsin yiu sīn buht "lìhng".
Could you check if this number's correct?	唔該查吓呢個號碼啱唔啱?
	Mh'gōi chàh háh nī go houhmáh ngāam-mh-ngāam?
Can I dial international (long distance) direct?	我可以直接打國際長途嗎?
	Ngóh hóyíh jihkjip dá gwokjai chèuhngtòuh ma?
Do I have to go through the switchboard?	駛唔駛經過總機呀?
	Sái-mh-sái gīnggwo júnggēi a?
Do I have to reserve my calls?	駛唔駛預訂時間呀?
	Sái-mh-sái yuhdihng sìhgaan a?
Could you dial this number for me, please?	唔該幫我打呢個電話。
	Mh'gōi bōng ngóh dá nī go dihnwá*.
Could you put me through to.../extension..., please?	唔該幫我轉 ... 號分機。
	Mh'gōi bōng ngóh jyún* houh fān'gēi.
I'd like to place a collect call to...	我想訂一個長途電話, 係對方俾錢嘅。
	Ngóh séung dehng yāt go chèuhngtòuh dihnwá*, haih deuifōng béi-chín* ge.
What's the charge per minute?	一分鐘嘅收費係幾多錢?
	Yāt fanjūng ge sāufai haih géidō chín*?
Have there been any calls for me?	有冇人打過電話俾我?
	Yáuh-móuh yàhn dá-gwo dihnwá* béi ngóh?

The conversation

Hello, this is...	喂, 我係 ...
	Wái, ngóh haih ...
Who is this, please?	請問邊位?
	Chíngmahn, bīnwái*
Is this...?	你係唔係呀... ?
	Néih haih-mh-haih a... ?
I'm sorry, I've dialed the wrong number	對唔住, 我打錯咗。
	Deui-mh'jyuh, ngóh dácho-jó.
I can't hear you.	我聽唔清楚。
	Ngóh dēng-mh'chīngchó.
I'd like to speak to...	... 喺唔喺度呀?
	... hái-mh-háidouh a?
Is there anybody who speaks English?	呢度有冇人識講英文呀?
	Nīdouh yáuh-móuh yàhn sīk góng Yīngmán* a?
Extension..., please	唔該幫我接 ... 分機。
	Mh'gōi bōng ngóh jip ... fān'gēi.
Operator, I've been cut off.	接線生, 我條線斷咗。
	Jipsin-sāng, ngóh tìuh sin tyúhn-jó.
This is the answering machine of...	呢個係... 嘅電話留言機。
	Nī go haih .... ge dihnwá* làuhyìhn-gēi.

有人打電話俾你	There's a phone call for you.
你要先撥 "零"	You have to dial "0" first.
唔該等一等。	One moment, please
冇人接電話。	There's no answer.
有人講緊。	The line's busy.
你想等吓嗎?	Do you want to hold?
唔好收線呀。	Don't hang up.
我而家幫你接線。	Connecting you.
你打錯喇。	You've got a wrong number.
佢唔喺（呢）度。	He's/she's not here right now.
佢 ... 點返嚟。	He'll/she'll be back at...

Could you ask him/her to call me back?	麻煩你叫佢覆我電話。
	Màhfàahn néih giu kéuih fūk ngóh dihnwá*.
My name's...	我叫做...
	Ngóh giujouh ...
My number's...	我嘅電話號碼係...
	Ngóh ge dihnwá* houhmáh haih ...
Could you tell him/her I called?	唔該話俾佢知我打過電話嚟。
	Mh'gōi wah béi kéuih jī ngóh dá-gwo dihnwá* làih.
I'll call him/her back tomorrow	我聽日再打電話俾佢。
	Ngóh tīngyaht joi dá dihnwá* béi kéuih.

Shopping

10.1 Shopping conversations   86

10.2 Food   88

10.3 Clothing and shoes   88

10.4 Photographs and video   90

10.5 At the hairdresser's   91

10 Shopping

● **All shops in Hong Kong** are open seven days a week. Corner shops are open from 7:00 a.m. till 10:00 p.m. Supermarkets are open from 9:00 a.m. till 9:00 p.m., in some places up to 10:00 p.m. Department stores are open from 11:00 a.m. till 9:00 p.m. There are two chains of convenience shops, 7-Eleven and Circle K, which open 24 hours a day all year round but they are more expensive.

雜貨舖 grocery shop	男裝服飾用品店 haberdashery	皮貨店 furrier
超級市場 supermarket	鐘錶舖 watches and clocks	花店 florist
百貨公司 department store	家庭用品 household goods	音響店 music shop (CDs, tapes, etc)
方便店 convenience shop	眼鏡舖 optician	
吃角子洗衣舖 coin-operated laundry/dry cleaner	服裝店 clothing shop	魚舖 fishmonger
生果舖 fruit shop	餅舖 bread/pastry shop	家用電器店 household appliances (white goods)
飛髮舖 barber's	報紙攤 newsstand	
書舖 book shop	理髮師 hairdresser	蔬菜水果店 greengrocer
玩具店 toy shop	攝影器材店 camera shop	香水店 perfumery
服飾店 costume jewelry	糖果店 confectioner's/cake shop	雪糕店 ice cream shop
肉舖 butcher's shop	藥材舖 herbalist's shop	歐式雜貨舖 delicatessen
鞋舖 footwear	運動用品（店） sporting goods	珠寶商 jeweller
街市 market	皮革用品（店） leather goods	美容店 beauty salon
金舖 goldsmith	藥房 pharmacy	洗衣店 laundry
文具店 stationery shop	床單檯布店 household linen shop	

10.1 Shopping conversations

Where can I get...?	邊度可以買到 … ? Bīndouh hóyíh máaih-dóu ... ?
When is this shop open?	呢間舖頭幾點開門? Nī gāan poutáu* géidím hōi-mùhn?
Could you tell me where the...department is?	請問, … 部門喺 / 響邊度? Chíngmahn, ... bouhmùhn hái/héung bīndouh?
Could you help me, please?	麻煩你幫我 … ? Màhfàahn néih bōng ngóh ....?

86

I'm looking for...	我揾 ... Ngóh wán ....
Do you sell English language newspapers?	你哋賣唔賣英文報紙呀? Néihdeih maaih-m̀h-maaih Yīngmàhn boují a?

買啲乜嘢呢?	Are you being served?

No, I'd like...	我想買 ... Ngóh séung máaih ...
I'm just looking, if that's all right.	我睇吓啫? Ngóh tái-háh jēk.

仲要啲乜嘢呢?	(Would you like) anything else?

Yes, I'd also like...	我仲要 ... Ngóh juhng yiu ...
No, thank you. That's all.	就係咁多,唔該。 Jauh haih gam dō, m̀h'gōi.
Could you show me...?	唔該攞 ... 俾我睇吓。 M̀h'gōi ló ... béi ngóh tái-háh.
I'd prefer...	我鐘意 ... Ngóh jūngyi ... ...
This is not what I'm looking for.	呢啲唔係我要嘅。 Nīdī m̀h'haih ngóh yiu ge.
Thank you, I'll keep looking.	冇所謂,我繼續揾。 Móuhsówaih, ngóh gaijuhk wán.
Do you have something...?	有冇 ... ? Yáuh-móuh ... ?
– less expensive?	平啲嘅? pèhng-dī ge?
– smaller?	細啲嘅? sai-dī ge?
– larger?	大啲嘅? daaih-dī ge?
I'll take this one.	我就要呢個。 Ngóh jauh yiu nī go.
Does it come with instructions?	有冇説明書? Yáuh-móuh syutmìhng-syū?
It's too expensive.	太貴了。 Taai gwai la.
I'll give you...	我俾你 ... 蚊。 Ngóh béi néih ... mān.
Could you keep this for me?	可唔可以幫我保存一吓。 Hó-m̀h-hóyíh bōng ngóh bóuchyùhn yat-háh.
I'll come back for it later.	我一陣間返嚟攞。 Ngóh yātjahn'gāan fāan-làih ló.

Shopping

10

| Do you have a bag for me, please? | 唔該俾個袋我。
Mh'gōi béi go dói* ngóh. |
| Could you gift wrap it, please? | 唔該幫我包成禮物。
Mh'gōi bōng ngóh bāau-sèhng láihmaht. |

對唔住，我哋冇呢種。	I'm sorry, we don't have that.
對唔住，賣晒喇。	I'm sorry, we're sold out.
對唔住，要等到 ... 先至有貨。	I'm sorry, it won't come back in until...
唔該去收銀處俾錢。	Please pay at the cash register.
我哋唔接受信用卡。	We don't accept credit cards.
我哋唔接受旅行支票。	We don't accept traveler's checks.

10.2 Food

I'd like a pound/kilo of...	我要一磅 / 公斤 ... Ngóh yiu yāt bohng/gūnggān ...
Could you cut it up for me, please?	唔該幫我切開。 Mh'gōi bōng ngóh chit-hōi.
Can I order it?	可唔可以訂購呀？ Hó-mh-hóyíh dehngkau a?
I'll pick it up tomorrow at...	我聽日 ... 嚟攞。 Ngóh tīngyaht ... làih ló.
Can you eat/drink this?	食唔食得㗎 / 飲唔飲得㗎？ Sihk-mh-sihkdāk ga / yám-mh-yámdāk ga?
What's in it?	入邊有啲乜嘢呀？ Yahpbihn yáuh dī mātyéh a?

10.3 Clothing and shoes

I saw something in the window	我喺 / 響櫥窗嗰度睇到啲嘢。 Ngóh hái/héung chyùhchēung gódouh tái-dóu dī yeh.
Shall I point it out?	我指俾你睇，好唔好呀？ Ngóh jí béi néih tái, hóu-mh-hóu a?
I'd like something to go with this	我想搵個配呢個嘅？ Ngóh séung wán go pui nī go ge.
Do you have shoes to match this?	有冇配（呢件衫）嘅鞋？ Yáuh-móuh pui (nī gihn sāam) ge hàaih?
I'm a size...in the U.S.	我著（美國）...號嘅。 Ngóh jeuk (méihgwok) ... houh ge.
Can I try this on?	我可以著吓嗎？ Ngóh hóyíh jeuk-háh ma?
Where's the fitting room?	試身室喺 / 響邊度呀？ Sisān-sāt hái/héung bīndouh a?

It (the garment) doesn't suit me.	呢件衫唔啱我。
	Nī gihn sāam m̀h'ngāam ngóh.
This is the right size.	呢個晒士啱啱好。
	Nī go sāaisí ngāam'ngāam hóu.
It doesn't look good on me.	我著起嚟唔好睇。
	Ngóh jeuk-héi-làih m̀h'hóu tái.
Do you have these in...size?	呢啲有冇 ... 號㗎?
	Nīdī yáuh-móuh ... houh ga?
The heel's too high/low.	鞋踭太高／矮了。
	Hàaihjāang taai gōu/ngái la.
Is this real leather?	係唔係真皮嚟㗎?
	Haih-m̀h-haih jānpéi làihga?
Is this genuine hide?	係唔係真嘅獸皮嚟㗎?
	Haih-m̀h-haih jān ge saupèih làihga?
I'm looking for a...for a...year-old child.	我想搵（個）... 送俾一個 ... 歲嘅細蚊仔。
	Ngóh séung wán (go)... sung béi yāt go ... seui ge saimānjái.
I'd like a...	我要一件...
	Ngóh yiu yāt gihn ...
– silk	真絲嘅
	jānsī ge
– cotton	綿織嘅
	mìhnjīk ge
– woolen	羊毛嘅
	yèuhngmòuh ge
– linen	麻布嘅
	màhbou ge
At what temperature should I wash it?	應該用幾暖嘅水嚟洗?
	Yīnggōi yuhng géi nyúhn ge séui làih sái?
Will it shrink in the wash?	會唔會縮水㗎?
	Wúih-m̀h-wúih sūkséui ga?

10

手洗	勿用熨斗熨	勿用乾衣機
Hand wash	Do not iron	Do not spin dry
乾洗	可用洗衣機洗	平放
Dry clean	Machine washable	Lay flat

At the cobbler

Could you mend these shoes?	呢對鞋可唔可以補呀?
	Nī deui hàaih hó-m̀h-hóyíh bóu a?
Could you resole/reheel these shoes?	呢對鞋可唔可以打掌／換踭呀?
	Nī deui hàaih hó-m̀h-hóyíh dá-jéung/wuhn-jāang a?
When will they be ready?	幾時可以嚟攞呀?
	Géisìh hóyíh làih ló a?
I'd like..., please	我想要 ...
	Ngóh séung yiu ...
– a can of shoe polish	一盒鞋油
	yāt hahp hàaihyáu*
– a pair of shoelaces	一對鞋帶
	yāt deui hàaihdáai*.

10 .4 Photographs and video

I'd like a film for this camera, please	我要一卷呢種相機嘅菲林，唔該。 Ngóh yiu yāt gyún nī júng séunggēi ge fēilám*, m̀h'gōi.
I'd like a cartridge, please	我要一卷菲林，唔該。 Ngóh yiu yāt gyún fēilám*, m̀h'gōi.
– a one twenty-four cartridge	一卷二十四嘅菲林，唔該。 Yāt gyún yih-sahp-sei jēung ge fēilám*.
– a slide film	一卷幻燈嘅菲林。 Yāt gyún waahndāng ge fēilám*.
– a movie cassette / videotape, please	我要一盒攝錄帶 / 錄影帶，唔該。 Ngóh yiu yāt hahp sipluhk-dáai*/ luhkyíng-dáai*, m̀h'gōi.
– color/black and white	彩色 / 黑白菲林。 chóisīk/hākbaahk fēilám*.
– 12/24/36 exposures	十二 / 二十四 / 三十六張嘅菲林 sahp-yih / yih-sahp-sei / sāam-sahp-luhk jēung ge fēilám*.
– ASA/DIN number	感光度數 gám'gwōng-douhsou.

Problems

Could you load the film for me, please?	唔該幫我將呢卷菲林裝入去。 M̀h'gōi bōng ngóh jēung nī gyún fēilám* jōng-yahp-heui.
Could you take the film out for me, please?	唔該幫我將菲林裝攞出嚟。 M̀h'gōi bōng ngóh jēung fēilám* ló-chēut-làih.
Should I replace the batteries?	駛唔駛換電池？ Sái-m̀h-sái wuhn dihnchìh?
Could you have a look at my camera, please?	唔該幫我睇吓相機有冇壞。 M̀h'gōi bōng ngóh tái-háh séunggēi yáuh-móuh waaih.
It's not working	壞咗 Waaih-jó
The...is broken	... 壞咗 ... waaih-jó
The film's jammed	菲林撳住咗 Fēilám* kīk-jyuh-jó.
The film's broken	菲林斷咗 Fēilám* tyúhn-jó.
The flash isn't working	閃光燈壞咗 Sím'gwōng-dāng waaih-jó

Processing and prints

I'd like to have this film developed/printed, please	我想沖晒呢卷菲林。 Ngóh séung chūngsaai nī gyún fēilám*.
I'd like...prints from each negative	每張相底我想晒 ... 張。 Múih jēung séungdái ngóh séung saai ... jēung.
glossy/matte	光面嘅 / 網面嘅 gwōngmín* ge / chàuhmín* ge

6 x 9 _____	六寸乘九寸嘅
	luhk chyun sìhng gáu chyun ge
I'd like to order reprints of these photos	我想晒呢啲相。
	Ngóh séung saai nīdī séung*.
I'd like to have this _____ photo enlarged	我想放大呢張相。
	Ngóh séung fongdaaih nī jēung séung*.
How much is processing? _	沖相要幾多錢？
	Chūng-séung yiu géidō chín*?
How much for printing? ____	晒相要幾多錢？
	Saai-séung yiu géidō chín*?
How much are the _____ reprints?	再晒要幾多錢？
	Joi saai yiu géidō chín*?
How much is it for _____ enlargement?	放大要幾多錢？
	Fongdaaih yiu géidō chín*?
When will they be ready? _	幾時可以攞相？
	Géisìh hóyíh ló-séung*?

10.5 At the hairdresser's

Do I have to make an _____ appointment?	駛唔駛預約呀？
	Sái-m̀h-sái yuhyeuk a?
Can I come in right now?	而家方唔方便入嚟呀？
	Yìhgā fōng-m̀h-fōngbihn yahp-làih n?
How long will I have _____ to wait?	要等幾耐呀？
	Yiu dáng géi noih a?
I'd like a shampoo/haircut _	我想洗頭／剪髮
	Ngóh séung sái-tàuh / jín-faat
I'd like a shampoo for _____ oily/dry hair, please	我想洗頭，我的頭髮好油／乾。
	Ngóh séung sái-tàuh . Ngóh dī tàuhfaat hóu yàuh/gōn.
I'd like an anti-dandruff _____ shampoo	我想洗頭，唔該用去頭皮嘅洗髮劑。
	Ngóh séung sái-tauh, m̀h'gōi yuhng heui tàuhpèih ge sáifaat-jāi.
I'd like a color-rinse _____ shampoo, please	我想洗頭，唔該用保色嘅洗髮劑。
	Ngóh séung sái-tauh, m̀h'gōi yùhng bóusīk ge sáifaat-jāi.
I'd like a shampoo with _____ conditioner, please	我想洗頭，唔該用帶二合一嘅洗髮劑。
	Ngóh séung sái-tauh, m̀h'gōi yuhng daai yih-sahp-yāt ge sáifaat-jāi.
I'd like highlights, please __	唔該加啲顯眼嘅顏色。
	Mh'gōi gā dī hín'ngáahn ge ngàahnsīk
Do you have a color _____ chart, please?	你哋有冇色譜呀？
	Néihdeih yáuh-móuh sīkpóu a?
I'd like to keep the _____ same color	我想保持一樣嘅顏色。
	Ngóh séung bóuchìh yātyeuhng ge ngàahnsīk.
I'd like it darker/lighter ____	我想深色／淺色一啲。
	Ngóh séung sāmsīk/chínsīk yāt-dī.
I'd like/I don't want _____ hairspray	我想／唔想噴定型膠。
	Ngóh séung/m̀h'séung pan dihngyìhng-gāau.
– gel _____	髮蠟
	faatlaahp

– lotion	洗髮露 sáifaat-louh
I'd like short bangs	我要短嘅劉海。 Ngóh yiu dyún ge làuhhói.
Not too short at the back	後面啲頭髮唔好剪得太短。 Hauhmihn dī tàuhfaat m̀h'hóu jín-dāk taai dyún.
Not too long	唔好剪得太長。 M̀h'hóu jín-dāk taai chèuhng.
I'd like it curly/not too curly	唔該幫我電攣啲／攣少少。 M̀h'gōi bōng ngóh dihn lyūn-dī／lyūn-díusíu.
I don't like it too curly	唔好電得太攣。 M̀h'hóu dihn-dāk taai lyūn.
I'd like a completely different style/a different cut	唔該幫我剪第二個髮型。 M̀h'gōi bōng ngóh jín daihyih go faatyìhng.
Could you turn the drier up/down a bit?	唔該將個吹風機開大啲／細啲。 M̀h'gōi jēung go chēuifūng-gēi hōi daaih-dī／sai-dī.
How do you want it cut?	你想點樣剪呀？ Néih séung dímyéung* jín a?

你想剪乜嘢髮型？	What style did you have in mind?
你想染成乜嘢顏色？	What color did you want it?
溫度啱唔啱呀？	Is the temperature all right for you?
你想睇啲乜嘢呀？	Would you like something to read?
你想飲啲乜嘢呀？	Would you like a drink?

I'd like a facial.	我想做個面膜。 Ngóh séung jouh go mihnmók*
– a manicure	我想修指甲。 Ngóh séung sāu jígaap.
– a massage	我想做個按摩。 Ngóh séung jouh go ngonmō.
Could you trim my..., please?	唔該幫我修一吓 ...。 M̀h'gōi bōng ngóh sāu yāt-háh ...
– bangs	劉海 làuhhói
– beard	鬍鬚 wùhsōu
– moustache	二撇雞 yihpitgāi
I'd like a shave, please	唔該幫我剃鬚。 M̀h'gōi bōng ngóh tai-sōu.
I'd like a wet shave, please	唔該幫我用水剃鬚。 M̀h'gōi bōng ngóh yuhng séui tai-sōu.

At the Tourist Information Center

11.1 Places of interest   94

11.2 Going out   96

11.3 Reserving tickets   97

11 At the Tourist Information Center

● **You can find a fair bit of travel information about Hong Kong** on the Internet. One useful site is

http://webserv1.discoverhongkong.com/login.html

The Hong Kong Tourist Information Center is located at the Star Ferry Pier in Kowloon and the Hong Kong Tourist Association is located at 99 Queens Road, Central. Their opening hours are 8:00 a.m. to 6:00 p.m. You are advised to go to the above centers and ask for information about tourist spots and accommodations. Your hotel information desk will introduce you to a range of tourist agencies which can plan and budget your holiday.

11 .1 Places of interest

Where's the Tourist Information Center, please?
請問，旅遊詢問處喺／響邊度呀？
Chíngmahn, léuihyàuh sēunmahn-chyu hái/héung bīndouh a?

Do you have a city map?
有冇本市地圖呀？
Yáuh-móuh búnsíh deihtòuh a?

Where is the museum?
博物館喺／響邊度呀？
Bokmaht-gwún hái/héung bīndouh a?

Where can I find a church?
邊度有教堂呀？
Bīndouh yáuh gaautòhng a?

Could you give me some information about...?
可唔可以俾我有關 ... 嘅資料呀？
Hó'm̀h-hóyíh béi ngóh yáu'gwāan ... ge jīlíu* a?

How much is this?
呢個幾多錢呀？
Nī go géidō chín* a?

What are the main places of interest?
有乜嘢主要嘅景點呀？
Yáuh mātyéh jyúyiu ge gíngdím a?

Could you point them out on the map?
唔該喺／響地圖上面指俾我睇吓。
M̀h'gōi hái/héung deihtòuh seuhngmihn jí béi ngóh tái-háh.

What do you recommend?
你推薦邊幾個景點呀？
Néih tēuijin bīn géi go gíngdím a?

We'll be here for a few hours.
我哋會喺／響（呢）度幾個鐘頭。
Ngóhdeih wúih hái/héung (nī)douh géi go jūngtàuh.

We'll be here for a day.
我哋會喺／響（呢）度（住）一日。
Ngóhdeih wúih hái (nī)douh (jyuh) yāt yaht.

We'll be here for a week.
我哋會喺／響（呢）度（住）一個星期。
Ngóhdeih wúih hái/héung (nī)douh (jyuh) yāt go sīngkèih.

We're interested in...
我哋對 ... 感興趣。
Ngóhdeih deui ... gám hingcheui.

Is there a scenic walk around the city?
有冇一條遊覽市容嘅路線呀？
Yáuh-móuh yāt tìuh yàuhláahm síhyùhng ge louhsin a?

How long does it take?
呢條路要行幾耐呀？
Nī tìuh louh yiu hàahng géi noih a?

Where does it start/end?	喺／響邊度開始／完? Hái/héung bīndouh hōichí/ yùhn?
Are there any boat trips?	有冇坐船旅遊嘅路線呀? Yáuh-móuh chóh-syùhn ge léuihyàuh louhsin a?
Where can we board?	喺／響邊度上船呀? Hái/héung bīndouh séuhng-syùhn a?
Are there any bus tours?	有冇坐旅遊車嘅路線呀? Yáuh-móuh chóh léuihyàuh-chē ge louhsin a?
Where do we get on?	喺／響邊度上車呀? Hái/héung bīndouh séuhng-chē a?
Is there a guide who speaks English?	有冇會講英文嘅導遊呀? Yáuh-móuh wúih góng Yīngmán* ge douhyàuh a?
What trips can we take around the area?	附近有冇景點可以去㗎? Fuhgahn yáuh-móuh gíngdím hóyíh heui ga?
Are there any excursions?	有冇短途嘅旅遊路線呀? Yáuh-móuh dyúntòuh ge léuihyàuh louhsin a?
Where do they go?	呢啲短途路線去邊度呀? Nīdī dyúntòuh louhsin heui bīndouh a?
We'd like to go to...	我哋想去 ... Ngóhdeih séung heui ...
How long is the excursion?	呢條短途路線有幾遠呀? Nītiuh dyúntòuh louhsin yáuh géi yúln a?
How long do we stay in...?	我哋喺／響 ... 幾耐呀? Ngóhdeih hái/héung ... géi noih a?
Are there any guided tours?	有冇啲旅行團包埋導遊㗎? Yauh móuh dī léuihhàhng-tyùhn bāau-màaih douhyàuh ga?
How much free time will we have there?	去到嗰度(我哋)有幾多自由活動嘅時間呀? Heui-dou gódouh (ngóhdeih) yáuh géidō jihyàuh wuhtduhng ge sìhgaan a?
We want to have a walk around.	我哋想喺附近行吓。 Ngóhdeih séung hái fuhgahn hàahng-háh.
Can we hire a guide?	我哋可唔可以請個導遊呀? Ngóhdeih hó-m̀h-hóyíh chéng go douhyàuh a?
What time does... open/close?	... 幾點開門／閂門? ... géidím hōi-mùhn / sāan-mùhn?
What days is...open/ closed?	... 邊日開門／閂門? ... bīnyaht hōi-mùhn / sāan-mùhn?
What's the admission price?	入場費幾多錢呀? Yahpchèuhng-fai géidō chín* a?
Is there a group discount?	團體有冇優惠呀? Tyùhntái yáuh-móuh yāuwaih a?
Is there a child discount?	細蚊仔有冇優惠呀? Saimānjái yáuh-móuh yāuwaih a?
Is there a discount for senior citizens?	老人有冇優惠呀? Lóuhyàhn yáuh-móuh yāuwaih a?
Can I take (flash) photos here?	呢度可唔可以用閃光燈呀? Nīdouh hó-m̀h-hóyíh yuhng sím'gwōng-dàng a?

Can I film here?	呢度可唔可以影錄像呀?
	Nídouh hó-m̀h-hóyíh yíng luhkjeuhng a?
Do you have any postcards of...?	有冇 ... 嘅明信片呀?
	Yáuh-móuh ... ge mìhngseun-pín* a?
Do you have an English...?	有冇英文嘅 ... 呀?
	Yáuh-móuh Yīngmán* ge ... a?
– catalog?	目錄?
	muhkluhk?
– program?	節目表?
	jitmuhk-bíu?
– brochure?	旅遊册?
	léuihyàuh-chaak?

11 .2 Going out

There aren't many bars, discos, late-night restaurants or coffee shops in Hong Kong. Foreigners tend to go to Lan Kwai Fong (Làahn'gwaifōng 蘭桂坊) at Central, Wanchai (Wāanjái 灣仔), and Tsim Sha Tsui (Jīmsājéui 尖沙嘴), although Causeway Bay (Tòhnglòhwāan 銅鑼灣) is another favorite spot. Try to get in to see a concert at the Hong Kong Stadium (Hēunggóng Táiyuhk-gwún 香港體育館), City Hall (Daaihwuihtòhng 大會堂) in Hong Kong or the Cultural Center (Hēunggóng Màhnfa Jūngsām 香港文化中心) in Tsim Sha Tsui.

Do you have this week's/month's entertainment guide?	有冇呢個星期／月嘅娛樂指南呀?
	Yáuh-móuh nīgo sīngkèih/yuht ge yùhlohk jí'nàahm a?
What's on tonight?	今晚有乜嘢好節目?
	Gāmmáahn yáuh mātyéh hóu jitmuhk?
We want to go to...	我哋想去 ...
	Ngóhdeih séung heui ... ...
What's playing at the cinema?	戲院做乜嘢戲呀?
	Heiyún jouh mātyéh hei a?
What sort of film is that?	係乜嘢片呀?
	Haih mātyéh pín* a?
– suitable for everyone	大人兒童都適宜觀看。
	Daaihyàhn yìhtùhng dōu sīkyìh gwūnhon.
– not suitable for people under 16	十六歲以下嘅兒童不宜觀看。
	Sahp-luhk seui yíhhah ge yìhtùhng bātyìh gwūnhon.
– original version	正版
	jingbáan
– subtitled	有字幕
	yáuh jihmohk
– dubbed	配音
	puiyām
What's on at the theater?	劇院做乜嘢戲?
	Kehk'yún jouh mātyéh hei?
What's on at the opera?	歌劇院做乜嘢歌劇?
	Gōkehk-yún jouh mātyéh gōkehk?
What's happening in the concert hall?	音樂廳有乜嘢表演?
	Yām'ngohk-tēng yáuh mātyéh bíuyín?

11

Where can I find a good disco around here?	附近邊度有好嘅 DISCO? Fuhgahn bīndouh yáuh hóu ge DISCO?
Is it members only?	係唔係會員先至入得呀? Haih-m̀h-haih wúi*yùhn sīnji yahp-dāk a?
Where can I find a good nightclub around here?	附近邊度有好嘅夜總會? Fuhgahn bīndouh yáuh hóu ge yehjúng-wúi*?
Is it evening wear only?	要著晚禮服嗎? Yiu jeuk máahn-láihfuhk ma?
Should I/we dress up?	我哋係唔係要著得好整齊呀? Ngóh/ Ngóhdeih haih-m̀h-haih yiu jeuk-dāk hóu jíngchàih a?
What time does the show start?	表演幾時開始? Bíuyín géisìh hōichí?
When's the next soccer match?	下一場足球賽係幾時呀? Hah yāt chèuhng jūkkàuh-choi haih géisìh a?
Who's playing?	邊隊對邊隊? Bīn deuih deui bīn deuih?
I'd like an escort for tonight.	今晚我想搵人陪我去。 Gammáahn ngóh séung wán yàhn pùih ngóh heui.

11 .3 Reserving tickets

Could you reserve some tickets for us?	唔該幫我哋訂幾張飛。 Mh'gōi bōng ngóhdeih dehng géi jēung fēi.
We'd like to book...seats/ a table for...	我想訂 ... 個人嘅位 / 檯。 Ngóh séung dehng ... go yàhn ge wái* / tói*
...front row seats/a table for...at the front	前排嘅位 / 喺前面 ... 個人嘅檯。 chìhn pàaih ge wái* / hái chìhnmihn .... go yàhn ge tói*.
...seats in the middle/ a table in the middle	中間嘅位 / 中間嘅檯。 jūnggāan ge wái* / jūnggāan ge tói*.
...back row seats/a table at the back	後面嘅位 / 後面嘅檯。 hauhmihn ge wái* / hauhmihn ge tói*.
Could I reserve...seats for the...o'clock performance?	我想訂 ... 張 ... 點開演嘅飛。 Ngóh séung dehng ... jēung ...dím hōiyín ge fēi.
Are there any seats left for tonight?	仲有冇今晚嘅飛呀? Juhng yáuh-móuh gāmmáahn ge fēi a?
How much is a ticket?	幾多錢一張飛呀? Géidō chín* yāt jēung fēi a?
When can I pick up the tickets?	幾時先至可以攞飛呀? Géisìh sīnjī hóyíh ló-fēi a?
I've got a reservation.	我訂咗飛嘞。 Ngóh dehng-jó fēi laak.
My name's...	我個名叫做 ... Ngóh go méng* giujouh ...

11

你想訂邊一場嘅飛呀?	Which performance do you want to reserve for?
你想坐喺／響邊度呀?	Where would you like to sit?
飛都賣晒喇。	Everything's sold out.
淨係有企嘅位。	It's standing room only.
我哋只係剩番樓廳嘅飛喇。	We've only got circle seats left.
我哋只係剩番上層樓廳嘅飛喇。	We've only got upper circle (way upstairs) seats left
我哋只係剩番樂隊席嘅飛喇。	We've only got orchestra seats left.
我哋只係剩番前排嘅飛喇。	We've only got front row seats left.
我哋只係剩番後排嘅飛喇。	We've only got seats left at the back.
你要幾多張飛?	How many seats would you like?
你要喺／響 ... 點之前嚟攞飛。	You'll have to pick up the tickets before...o'clock.
呢張係你嘅位。	This is your seat.
(唔好意思), 你坐錯位嘞。	You are in the wrong seat.

Entertainment

12.1 Sporting questions   100

12.2 By the waterfront   100

12.3 Sightseeing   102

12.4 Nightlife   103

12.5 Cultural performances   103

12 Entertainment

12.1 Sporting questions

Where's the stadium/ gymnasium?	體育館喺/響邊度呀? Táiyuhk-gwún hái/héung bīndouh a?
I'd like to see a ball game.	我想去睇打波。 Ngóh séung heui tái dábō.
Can we go to see a ... game?	我哋可唔可以去睇 ... 比賽呀? Ngóhdeih hó-m̀h-hóyíh heui tái ... béichōi a?
I'd like to see a ... game.	我想去睇 ... 比賽。 Ngóh séung heui tái ... béichoi.
– soccer	足球 jūkkàuh
– basketball	籃球 làahm-kàuh
– badminton	羽毛球 yúhmòuh-kàuh
– volleyball	排球 pàaihkàuh
– table tennis	乒乓波 bīngbāng-bō
– tennis	網球 móhngkàuh
– baseball	棒球 páahngkàuh
– softball	壘球 lèuihkàuh
When does the game begin?	比賽幾時開始? Béichoi géisìh hōichí?
Which teams are going to play?	邊隊同邊隊打? Bīn deuih tùhng bīn deuih dá?
What's the score?	比數係幾多呀? Béisou haih géidō a?
I've won.	我贏咗。 Ngóh yèhng-jó.
I've lost	我輸咗。 Ngóh syū-jó.
We're even.	(我哋) 打和。 (Ngóhdeih) dá-wòh

12.2 By the waterfront

Is it far (to walk) to the sea?	呢度去海邊有幾遠呀? Nīdouh heui hóibīn yáuh géi yúhn a?
Is there a...around here?	呢度有冇 ... ? Nīdouh yáuh-móuh ... ?
– a swimming pool	游水池 yàuhséui-chìh

– a sandy beach	沙灘 / 海灘	
	sātāan/hóitāan	
Are there any rocks here?	呢度有冇石頭呀?	
	Nīdouh yáuh-móuh sehktàuh a?	
When's high/low tide?	幾時潮漲 / 潮退?	
	Géisìh chìuhjeung/chìuhteui?	
What's the water temperature?	水嘅溫度係幾多度?	
	Séui ge wāndouh haih géidō douh?	
Is it deep here?	呢度啲水深唔深呀?	
	Nīdouh dī séui sām-m̀h-sām a?	
Is it safe (for children) to swim here?	(細蚊仔)喺呢度游水安唔安全㗎?	
	(Saimānjái) hái nīdouh yàuhséui ngōn-m̀h-ngōnchyùhn ga?	
Are there any ...?	呢度有冇...?	
	Nīdouh yáuh-móuh ...?	
– current	急流	
	gāplàuh	
– sharks	鯊魚	
	sāyùh	
– jellyfish	白蚱	
	baahkja	
What does that flag mean?	嗰枝旗係乜嘢意思呀?	
	Gó jī kèih haih mātyéh yisī a?	
What does that buoy mean?	嗰個浮標係乜嘢意思呀?	
	Gó go fàuhbiu haih mātyéh yisī a?	
Is there a lifeguard on duty?	呢度有冇救生員值班?	
	Nīdouh yáuh móuh gausāang-yùhn jihkbāan?	
Is camping on the beach allowed?	海灘准唔准露營?	
	Hóitāan jéun-m̀h-jéun louhyìhng?	
Can we light a fire?	我哋可以點火嗎?	
	Ngóhdeih hóyíh dím-fó ma?	

危險	呢度唔准游水 / 釣魚。
Danger	No swimming/fishing

Where can I get ...?	邊度有...?	
	Bīndouh yáuh ... ?	
– sun lotion	太陽油 / 防晒油	
	taaiyèuhng-yàuh / fòhngsaai-yàuh	
– a bathing suit	泳衣	
	wihng-yī	
– a chair	凳	
	dang	
– a beach umbrella	太陽遮	
	taaiyèuhng-jē	
– a towel	毛巾	
	mòuhgān	
Where can I have a shower?	邊度可以沖涼呀?	
	Bīndouh hóyíh chūnglèuhng a?	

I'd like to visit the countryside.	我想去鄉下睇吓。 Ngóh séung heui hēunghá* tái-háh.
I'd like to visit	我想去睇吓 ... Ngóh séung heui tái-háh ...
– Stanley Market	赤柱 chekchyúh
– Golden Mile (Nathan Road)	彌敦道 Nèihdēun Douh
– Hollywood Road ("Cat Street")	荷理活道 Hòhléihwuht Douh
– Peak Pavilion (Victoria Peak)	老欄亭 Lóuhchan-tìhng
– Happy Valley (Hong Kong Jockey Club)	快活谷 Faaiwuht-gūk
– Mid-Level Escalator	半山自動扶梯 Bunsāan Jihduhng Fùhtāi
– Repulse Bay	淺水灣 Chínséui-wāan
– Ocean Park	海洋公園 Hóiyèuhng Gūngyún*
– Aberdeen (Floating Restaurant)	香港仔 Hēunggóngjái
– Wong Tai Sin (Daoist temple)	黃大仙 Wòhng Daaihsīn
– Hong Kong Conference and Exhibition Center	香港會展中心 Hēunggóng Wuih-jín Jūngsām
– Hong Kong Museum of Art	香港藝術館 Hēunggóng Ngaihseuht-gwún
– Hong Kong Museum of History and Culture	香港歷史文化博物館 Hēunggóng Lihksí Màhnfa Bokmaht-gwún
– The Bolin Temple	寶蓮寺 Bólìhn-jí
– Hakka Museum	三棟屋 Sāamduhng-ngūk
– Kowloon Walled-city Park	九龍寨城公園 Gáulùhng Jaaihsìhng Gūngyún*
– China Folk Culture village (in Shenzhen)	中國文化村 Jūnggwok Màhnfa chyūn
– Lisbon Casino (in Macao)	葡京賭場 Pòuhgīng Dóuchèuhng
– Ruins of St. Paul's Cathedral (in Macao)	大三巴牌坊 Daaihsāambā Pàaihfōng
– Temple of Mahjou (in Macao)	媽祖廟 Mājóu-míu*

12.4 Nightlife

I'd like to go to... — 我想去 ...
Ngóh séung heui ...

– Temple Street — 廟街
Miuh Gāai

– Women's Street — 女人街
Néuihyán* Gāai

– The Lanes — 利源東 / 西街
Leihyùhn Dūng/Sāi Gāai

– Hong Kong Culture Center — 香港文化中心
Hēunggóng Màhnfa Jūngsām

– Hong Kong City Hall — 香港大會堂
Hēunggóng Daaiwuihtòhng

– Hung Hom Stadium — 紅磡體育館
Hùhngham Táiyuhk-gwún

– Wanchai — 灣仔
Wāanjái

– Soho
(in Causeway Bay) — 蘇豪
Sōuhòuh

Where's Lan Gwai Fong? — 蘭桂坊喺 / 響邊度呀？
Làahn'gwaifōng hái/héung bīndouh a?

Where's the bar? — 酒吧喺 / 響邊度呀？
Jáubā hái/héung bīndouh a?

Please bring me a beer. — 俾杯啤酒我，唔該。
Béi būi bējáu ngóh, m̀h'gōi.

I'd like a glass of whisky — 我想要杯威士忌。
Ngóh séung yiu būi wāisihgéi.

straight — 唔加冰
M̀h'gā-bīng

on the rocks — 加冰
gā-bīng

12.5 Cultural performances

What's there to do in the evening? — 晚黑有啲乜嘢娛樂節目呀？
Máahnhāk yáuh dī mātyéh yùhlohk jitmuhk a?

Is there a disco here? — 呢度有冇 DISCO 呀？
Nīdouh yáuh-móuh DISCO a ?

I'd like to see ... — 我想睇
Ngóh séung tái ...

– Peking Opera — 京劇
Gīngkehk

– Cantonese opera — 粵劇
Yuhtkehk

– an acrobatic performance — 雜技表演
jaahpgeih bíuyín

– a song and dance show — 歌舞
gōmóuh

– martial arts performance — 武術表演
móuhseuht bíuyín

– folk dances _____ 民間舞蹈
màhn'gāan móuhdouh

– ballet _____ 芭蕾舞
bālèuih-móuh

– a Chinese classical _____ 國樂演奏
music concert Gwokngohk yínjau

– a magic show _____ 魔術表演
mōseuht bíuyín

– a movie _____ 電影
dihnyíng

– a Chinese movie _____ 中國電影
Jūnggwok dihnyíng

– a kungfu/action movie __ 武俠片 / 動作片
móuhhahp-pín* / duhngjok-pín*

I'd like to go to a concert. _ 我想去聽音樂會。
Ngóh séung heui tēng yām'ngohk-wúi*

I'd like to go to a singing _ 我想去聽演唱會。
recital. Ngóh séung heui tēng yíncheung-wúi*

Are there English subtitles? 有冇英文字幕?
Yáuh-móuh Yīngmàhn jih'mohk?

Are there any tickets for __ 有冇今晚嘅飛?
tonight's show? Yáuh-móuh gāmmáahn ge fēi?

Must tickets be _____ 係唔係一定要提前買飛呀?
purchased in advanced? Haih-m̀h-haih yātdihng yiu tàihchìhn máaih-
fēi a?

How much are the least _ 最平嘅座位幾多錢呀?
expensive seats? Jeui pèhng ge johwái* géidō chín* a?

How much are front row __ 前排嘅座位幾多錢呀?
seats? Chìhnpàaih ge johwái* géidō chín* a?

May I have a program? __ 唔該俾份節目表我。
M̀h'gōi béi fahn jitmuhk-bíu ngóh

Sickness

13.1 Call (get) the doctor   106

13.2 Patient's ailments   106

13.3 The consultation   107

13.4 Medication and prescriptions   110

13.5 At the dentist's   111

13.1 Call (get) the doctor

● **In Hong Kong,** if you become ill or need emergency treatment, you can call 999. For foreign tourists, the first treatment is free at the Emergency Unit. Subsequently you pay at the tourist rate. There are special departments for foreign nationals in many large hospitals where they have better facilities and you are expected to pay more for the treatment.

The procedures are: first, go directly to Casualty to register; second, have your illness treated; and third, settle the bill. Of course, in critical cases, treatment will come first and then registration and payment later.

Could you call (get) a _____ doctor quickly, please?	唔該快啲幫我搵個醫生。 M̀h'gōi faai-dī bōng ngóh wán go yīsāng.
When does the doctor _____ have office hours?	醫生幾點開始睇病? Yīsāng géidím hōichí tái-behng?
When can the doctor _____ come?	醫生幾時可以嚟? Yīsāng géisìh hóyíh làih?
Could I make an _____ appointment to see the doctor?	我想預約睇病。 Ngóh séung yuhyeuk tái-behng.
I've got an appointment _____ to see the doctor at...o'clock	我預約咗 ... 點睇病。 Ngóh yuhyeuk-jó ... dím tái-behng.
Which doctor is on _____ night/weekend duty?	夜晚／周末邊位醫生當值? Yehmáahn/jāumuht bīn wái* yīsāng dōngjihk?
Which pharmacy is on _____ night/weekend duty?	夜晚／周末邊間藥房開? Yehmáahn/jāumuht bīn gāan yeuhkfòhng hōi?

13.2 Patient's ailments

I don't feel well. _____	我覺得有啲唔舒服。 Ngóh gokdāk yáuhdī m̀h'syūfuhk.
I'm dizzy. _____	我覺得頭暈。 Ngóh gokdāk tàuhwàhn.
I'm ill _____	我唔舒服。 Ngóh m̀h'syūfuhk.
I feel sick (nauseous). _____	我有啲作嘔。 Ngóh yáuhdī jok'ngáu.
I've got a cold. _____	我傷風。 Ngóh sēungfūng.
I've got diarrhea. _____	我肚屙。 Ngóh tóu'ngō.
I have trouble breathing. _____	我呼吸有啲困難。 Ngóh fūkāp yáuhdī kwannàahn.
I feel tired all over. _____	我全身酸軟冇力。 Ngóh chyùhnsān syūn'yúhn móuhlihk.

I've burnt myself.	我燒傷咗自己。 Ngóh sīu-sēung-jó jihgéi.
It hurts here.	呢度痛。 Nīdouh tung.
I've been sick (vomited).	我嘔過。 Ngóh ngáu-gwo.
I'm running a temperature of...degrees.	我發燒, ... 度。 Ngóh faatsīu, ... douh.
I've been...	我 ... Ngóh ...
– stung by a wasp.	俾黃蜂刮親。 béi wòhngfūng gāt-chān.
– stung by an insect.	俾蟲咬親。 béi chùhng ngáauh-chān.
– stung by a jellyfish.	俾白蚱整親。 béi baahkja jíng-chān.
– bitten by a dog.	俾狗咬親。 béi gáu ngáauh-chān.
– bitten by a snake.	俾蛇咬親。 béi sèh ngáauh-chān.
I've cut myself.	我割親自己。 Ngóh got-chān jihgéi.
I've grazed/scratched myself.	我刮傷自己。 Ngóh gwaat sēung jiligéi.
I've had a fall.	我跌咗一交。 Ngóh dit-jó yāt gāau.
I've sprained my ankle.	我拗親腳踭。 Ngóh náau-chān góulgaung.
Could I have a female doctor, please?	可唔可以幫我搵個女醫生? Hó-ṁh-hóyíh bōng ngóh wán go néuih yīsāng?
I'd like the morning-after pill.	我想買行房後第二日用嘅避孕丸。 Ngóh séung máaih hàhng-fòhng hauh daih-yih yaht yuhng ge beihyahn-yún.

13.3 The consultation

你邊度唔舒服?	What seems to be the problem?
你呢個病情已經有咗幾耐喇?	How long have you had these complaints?
你以前有過嘅呢病嗎?	Have you had this trouble before?
有冇發燒呀? 幾多度?	Do you have a temperature? What is it?
唔該你解開件衫。	Open your shirt, please
唔該除咗上面件衫。	Strip to the waist, please .
你可以喺 / 響呢度除衫。	You can undress there

107

捲起左邊 / 右邊衫袖啦。	Roll up your left/right sleeve, please
唔該你瞓低。	Lie down here, please
噉樣痛唔痛呀?	Does this hurt?
深呼吸。	Breathe deeply.
擘大個嘴。	Open your mouth.

Patients' medical history

I'm a diabetic.
我有糖尿病。
Ngóh yáuh tòhngniuh-behng.

I have a heart condition.
我有心臟病。
Ngóh yáuh sāmjohng-behng.

I'm asthmatic.
我有哮喘病。
Ngóh yáuh hāauchyún-behng.

I'm allergic to...
我對 ... 過敏。
Ngóh deui ... gwomáhn.

I'm...months pregnant.
我有咗 ... 個月身紀。
Ngóh yáuh-jó ... go yuht sān'géi.

I'm on a diet.
我節緊食。
Ngóh jit-gán-sihk.

I'm on medication/ the pill.
我食緊避孕丸。
Ngóh sihk-gán beihyahn-yún.

I've had a heart attack once before.
我以前試過一次心臟病發作。
Ngóh yíhchìhn si-gwo yāt chi sāmjohng-behng faatjok.

I've had a(n)...operation.
我以前做個 ... 手術。
Ngóh yíhchìhn jouh-gwo ... sáuseuht.

I've been ill recently.
我最近病過一次。
Ngóh jeuigahn behng-gwo yāt chi.

I've got a stomach ulcer.
我有胃潰瘍。
Ngóh yáuh waih-kwúiyèuhng.

I've got my period.
我啱啱嚟月經。
Ngóh ngāamngāam làih yuhtgīng.

你對乜嘢過敏?	Do you have any allergies?
你而家食乜嘢藥?	Are you on any medication?
你係唔係節緊食?	Are you on a diet?
你係唔係有咗身紀呀?	Are you pregnant?
你有冇打過破傷風針呀?	Have you had a tetanus injection?

Sickness

13

The diagnosis

冇乜事，唔駛擔心。	It's nothing serious.
你嘅 ... 斷咗。	Your...is broken.
你扭傷咗 ... 。	You've got a sprained...
你嘅 ... 扯傷咗	You've got a torn...
你感染到 ... 。	You've got an infection.
你嘅 ... 發炎嘞。	You've got some inflammation.
你有盲腸炎。	You've got appendicitis.
你感染到支氣管炎。	You've got bronchitis
你有性病。	You've got a venereal disease.
你感冒嘞。	You've got the flu.
你有過輕微嘅心臟病發作。	You've had a mild heart attack.
你係肺炎。	You've got pneumonia.
你係胃炎 / 胃潰瘍。	You've got gastritis/an ulcer.
你扯傷咗肌肉。	You've pulled a muscle.
妳嘅陰道發炎。	You've got a vaginal infection.
你食嘢中毒。	You've got food poisoning.
你中暑。	You've got sunstroke.
你對 ... 過敏。	You're allergic to...
妳懷孕喇。	You're pregnant.
我幫你驗血 / 尿 / 大便。	I'd like to have your blood/urine/stools tested
要挐傷口。	It needs stitches.
我將你介紹俾專科醫生。	I'm referring you to a specialist.
我而家送你入醫院。	I'm sending you to the hospital
你要照X光。	You'll need some x-rays taken.
唔該你喺 / 響候診室嗰度等。	Could you wait in the waiting room, please?
你需要做手術。	You'll need an operation.

I need something for diarrhea.	我要啲肚屙嘅藥。 Ngóh yiu dī yī tóuh'ngō ge yeuhk.
I need something for a cold.	我要啲醫感冒嘅藥。 Ngóh yiu dī gámmouh ge yeuhk.
Is it contagious?	會唔會傳染俾人㗎? Wúih-m̀h-wúih chyùhn'yím béi yàhn ga?

How long do I have to stay ...?	我要 ... 幾耐呀? Ngóh yiu ... géi noih a?
– in bed	瞓床 fan-chòhng
– in the hospital	喺 / 響醫院住 hái/héung yīyún jyuh
Do I have to go on a special diet?	駛唔駛食特別嘅營養餐呀? Sái-m̀h-sái sihk dahkbiht ge yìhngyéuhng-chāan a?
Am I allowed to travel?	我可以去旅行嗎? Ngóh hóyíh heui léuihhàhng ma?
Can I make another appointment?	我可以再預約個時間嗎? Ngóh hóyíh joi yuhyeuk go sìhgaan ma?
When do I have to come back for another consultation?	我幾時再返嚟復診? Ngóh géisìh joi fāan-làih fūkchán?
I'll come back tomorrow.	我聽日返嚟。 Ngóh tīngyaht fāan-làih.
How do I take this medicine?	呢種藥點樣食? Nī júng yeuhk dímyéung* sihk?

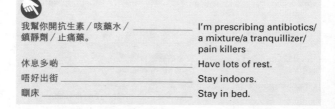

你聽日 / ... 日再返嚟復診。	Come back tomorrow/in... days' time.

13.4 Medication and prescriptions

How many pills/drops/spoonfuls each time?	每次食幾多粒 / 滴 / 羹? Múih chi sihk géidō lāp/dihk/gāng?
How many injections each time?	每次打幾針? Múih chi dá géi jām?
How many times a day?	一日食幾多次? Yāt yaht sihk géidō chi?
I've forgotten my medication	我唔記得食藥。 Ngóh m̀h'geidāk sihk-yeuhk
At home I take...	喺 / 響屋企我食 ... Hái/héung ngūkkéi ngóh sihk ...
Could you write a prescription for me, please?	唔該幫我開張藥單。 M̀h'gōi bōng ngóh hōi jēung yeuhkdāan.

我幫你開抗生素 / 咳藥水 / 鎮靜劑 / 止痛藥。	I'm prescribing antibiotics/ a mixture/a tranquillizer/ pain killers
休息多啲	Have lots of rest.
唔好出街	Stay indoors.
瞓床	Stay in bed.

Sickness

13

藥丸	呢種藥要全部食完。	打針
pills	Finish the prescription.	injections
溶喉／響水（啊）度		藥膏
dissolve in water	成粒吞	ointment
飯前	swallow (whole)	每日食 ... 次
before meals	外用	...times a day
飯後	external use only	食 ... 日
after meals	羹／茶羹	for...days
藥丸	spoonful/teaspoonful	食（藥）／
tablets	每 ... 鐘頭／小時	飲（藥水）
滴劑	every...hours	take
drops	搽	
呢種藥會影響你揸車。	rub on	
This medication impairs your driving.		

13 .5 At the dentist's

Do you know a good dentist?	你識唔識得好嘅牙醫呀？ Néih sīk-m̀h-sīkdāk hóu ge ngàhyī a?
Could you make a dentist's appointment for me?	唔該幫我預約個牙醫。 M̀h'gōi bōng ngóh yuhyeuk go ngàhyī.
It's urgent.	好緊急㗎。 Hóu gán'gāp ga
Can I come in today, please.	可唔可以今日嚟呀？ Hó-m̀h-hóyíh gāmyaht làih a?
I have a (terrible) toothache.	我隻牙痛得好犀害。 Ngóh jek ngàh tung dāk hóu lcihhoih.
Could you prescribe/ give me a painkiller?	可唔可以開啲止痛藥俾我食呀？ Hó-m̀h-hóyíh hōi dī jítung-yeuhk bèi ngóh sihk a?
I've got a broken tooth.	我隻牙撞崩咗。 Ngóh jek ngàh johng-bāng-jó.
My filling's come out.	我補牙啲 filling 甩咗出嚟。 Ngóh bóu'ngàh dī FILLING lat-jó chēut-làih.
I've got a broken crown.	我隻鑲金／銀牙撞爛咗。 Ngóh jek sēung-gām/ngàhn-ngàh johng-laahn-jó.
I'd like a local anaesthetic.	唔該幫我打麻藥。 M̀h'gōi bōng ngóh dá màhyeuhk.
I don't want a local anaesthetic.	我唔想打麻藥。 Ngóh m̀h'séung dá màhyeuhk.
I'm giving you a local anaesthetic.	我而家幫你打麻藥。 Ngóh yìhgā bōng néih dá màhyeuhk.
Could you do a temporary repair?	可唔可以幫我臨時補一補呀？ Hó-m̀h-hóyíh bōng ngóh làhmsìh bóuyātbóu ngàh a?
I don't want this tooth pulled.	我唔想擝呢隻呀。 Ngóh m̀h'séung māng nī jek ngàh.
My denture is broken.	我副假牙撞爛咗。 Ngóh fu gá'ngàh johng-làahn-jó.

Sickness

13

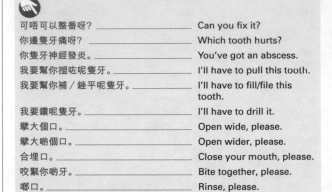

可唔可以整番呀?	Can you fix it?
你邊隻牙痛呀?	Which tooth hurts?
你隻牙神經發炎。	You've got an abscess.
我要幫你擳咗呢隻牙。	I'll have to pull this tooth.
我要幫你補／銼平呢隻牙。	I'll have to fill/file this tooth.
我要鑽呢隻牙。	I'll have to drill it.
擘大個口。	Open wide, please.
擘大啲個口。	Open wider, please.
合埋口。	Close your mouth, please.
咬緊你啲牙。	Bite together, please.
嗽口。	Rinse, please.
仲痛唔痛呀?	Does it hurt still?

In trouble

14.1 Asking for help   114

14.2 Loss   115

14.3 Accidents   115

14.4 Theft   116

14.5 Missing person   116

14.6 The police   117

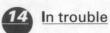

14 In trouble

14.1 Asking for help

Help!	救命啊! Gau'mehng a!
Get help quickly!	快啲揾人嚟幫手! Faai-dī wán-yàhn làih bōng-sáu!
Fire!	火燭啊! Fójūk a!
Police!	叫警察! Giu gíngchaat!
Get a doctor!	揾醫生! Wán yīsāng!
Quick/Hurry!	快啲! Faai-dī!
Danger!	危險! Ngàihhím!
Watch out!/ Be careful!	小心呀! Síusām a!
Stop!	唔好郁! M̀h'hóu yūk!
Get your hands off me!	攞開你隻手! Ló-hōi néih jek sáu!
Let go!	開放我! Fong-hōi ngóh!
Stop thief!	捉賊呀! Jūk chaak* a!
Could you help me, please?	唔該幫吓我吖. M̀h'gōi bōng-háh ngóh ā.
Where's the police station/emergency exit/ fire escape?	警察局 / 消防道 / 太平梯喺 / 響邊度呀? Gíngchaat-gúk*/ sīufòhng-douh/ taaipìhng-tāi hái/héung bīndouh a?
Where's the nearest fire extinguisher?	最近嘅滅火器喺 / 響邊度呀? Jeuikáhn ge mihtfó-hei hái/héung bīndouh a?
Call the fire department!	叫火燭車! Giu fójūk-chē!
Call the police!	叫警察! Giu gíngchaat!
Call an ambulance!	叫救傷車! Giu gausēung-chē!
Where's the nearest phone?	最近嘅公眾電話喺 / 響邊度呀? Jeuikáhn ge gūngjung dihnwá* hái/héung bīndouh a?
Could I use your phone?	可唔可以借你個電話用吓呀? Hó-m̀h-hóyíh je néih go dihnwá* yuhng-háh a?
What's the emergency number?	緊急號碼係幾多號呀? Gán'gāp houhmáh haih géidō houh a?
What's the number for the police?	警察局嘅電話係幾多號呀? Gíngchaat-gúk* ge dihnwá* haih géidō houh a?

14.2 Loss

I've lost my wallet/purse. — 我唔見咗銀包。
Ngóh m̀h'gin-jó ngàhnbāau.

I lost my...here yesterday. — 我琴日喺／響呢度唔見咗 ...
Ngóh kàhmyaht hái/héung nīdouh m̀h'gin-jó ...

I left my...here. — 我喺／響呢度唔見咗我嘅 ...
Ngóh hái/héung nīdouh m̀h'gin-jó ngóh ge ...

Did you find my...? — 你搵唔搵到我嘅 ... ?
Néih wán-m̀h-wán-dóu ngóh ge ... ?

It was right here. — 我記得係放喺／響呢度㗎。
Ngóh geidāk haih fong hái/héung nīdouh ga.

It's very valuable. — 好值錢㗎。
Hóu jihkchín* ga.

Where's the lost and — 失物待領處喺／響邊度呀？
found office? Sātmaht doihlíhng-chyu hái/héung bīndouh a?

14.3 Accidents

There's been an accident. — （呢度）發生咗意外。
(Nnīdouh) faatsāng jó yi'ngoih.

Someone's fallen into — 有人跌咗落水！
the water. Yáuh yàhn dit-jó lohk séui!

There's a fire. — 火燭喇！
Fójūk la!

Is anyone hurt? — 有冇人受傷呀？
Yáuh-móuh yàhn sauhsēung a?

Nobody has been injured. — 冇人受傷。
Móuh yàhn sauh-sēung.

Someone has been — 有人受傷。
injured. Yáuh yàhn sauhsēung.

Someone's still trapped — 有人仲喺車入邊。
inside the car. Yáuh yàhn juhng hái chē yahpbihn.

It's not too bad. — 唔係傷得太重。
M̀h'haih sēung-dāk taai chúhng.

Don't worry. — 唔駛擔心。
M̀h'sái dāamsām.

Leave everything the — 唔好郁任何嘢嘅。
way it is, please. M̀h'hóu yūk yahmhòh ge yéh.

I want to talk to the — 我要先同警察講。
police first. Ngóh yiu sīn tùhng gíngchaat góng.

I want to take a photo — 我要先影張相。
first. Ngóh yiu sīn yíng jēung séung*.

Here's my name and — 呢個係我嘅名同地址。
address. Nī go haih ngóh ge méng* tùhng deihjí.

May I have your name — 唔該俾你個名同地址我。
and address? M̀h'gōi béi néih go méng* tùhng deihjí ngóh.

Could I see your identity — 唔該俾我睇吓你嘅身份証／保險單。
card/your insurance M̀h'gōi béi ngóh tái-háh néih ge sānfán-jing /
papers? bóuhím-dāan.

In trouble

14

Will you act as a witness?	你願意做証人嗎? Néih yuhnyi jouh jing'yàhn ma?
I need this information for insurance purposes.	我嘅保險公司需要呢啲資料。 Ngóh ge bóuhím gūngsī sēuiyiu nīdī jīlíu*.
Are you insured?	你有冇買保險呀? Néih yáuh-móuh máaih bóuhím a?
Third party or all inclusive?	你買嘅係第三者保險定係全保? Néih máaih ge haih daihsāmjé bóuhím dihnghaih chyùhnbóu?
Could you sign here, please?	唔該你喺／響呢度簽個名。 M̀h'gōi néih hái/héung nīdouh chīm go méng*.

14.4 Theft

I've been robbed.	我俾人搶劫。 Ngóh béi yàhn chéunggip.
My...has been stolen.	我啲 ... 俾人偷咗。 Ngóh dī ... béi yàhn tāu-jó.
My car's been broken into.	我架車俾人繳開咗。 Ngóh gā chē béi yàhn giuh-hōi-jó.

14.5 Missing person

I've lost my child.	我個仔／女走失咗。 Ngóh go jái/néui* jáu-sāt-jó.
Could you help me find him/her?	你可唔可以幫我搵吓佢呀? Néih hó-m̀h-hóyíh bōng ngóh wán-háh kéuih a?
Have you seen a lost child?	你有冇見過一個蕩失路嘅細蚊仔呀? Néih yáuh-móuh gin'gwo yāt go dohng-sāt-louh ge saimānjái a?
He's/she's...years old	佢 ... 歲。 Kéuih ... seui.
He/she's got...hair	佢嘅頭髮係 ... 嘅。 Kéuih ge tàuhfaat haih ... sīk ge.
short/long	短／長 dyún/chèuhng
blond/red/brown/black/grey	金色／紅色／咖啡色／黑色／灰色 gāmsīk/hùhngsīk/gāfēsīk/hāksīk/fūisīk
curly/straight/ frizzy	攣／直／細圈 lyūn/jihk/sai'hyūn
...in a ponytail	梳馬尾嘅 sō máhméih ge
...in braids	梳辮嘅 sō bīn ge
...in a bun	梳髻嘅 sō gai ge
He's/she's got blue/brown/green eyes.	佢對眼係藍色嘅／咖啡色嘅／綠色嘅。 Kéuih deui ngáahn haih làahmsīk ge / gāfēsīk ge / luhksīk ge.
He/she's wearing...	佢著住 ... Kéuih jeuk-jyuh ...

In trouble

14

swimming trunks/ hiking boots	游水褲 / 旅行鞋 yàuhséui-fu / léuihhàhng-hàaih.
with/without glasses	戴 / 冇戴眼鏡。 daai / móuh daai ngáahn'géng
carrying a bag	手拎住個袋。 Sáu līng-jyuh go dói*
He/She is tall/short.	佢生得高 / 矮。 Kéuih sāang-dāk gōu / ngái.
This is a photo of him/her.	呢張係佢嘅相。 Nī jēung haih kéuih ge séung*
He/she must be lost	佢一定係蕩失咗。 Kéuih yātdihng haih dohngsāt-jó.

14.6 The police

An arrest

唔該俾我睇吓你嘅駕駛執照。	Your (vehicle) documents, please.
你開快車。	You were speeding.
呢度唔準泊車。	You're not allowed to park here.
你冇放錢喺 / 響咪子機入面。	You haven't put money in the parking meter.
你嘅車頭燈 / 車尾燈唔著。	Your lights aren't working.
呢個係 ... 罰款。	That's a ...fine.

I don't speak Cantonese.	我唔識講廣東話。 Ngóh m̀h'sīk góng Gwóngdūng-wá*
I didn't see the sign.	我睇唔到路牌。 Ngóh tái'm̀h-dóu louhpáai*
I don't understand what it says.	我睇唔明上面講乜嘢。 Ngóh tái'm̀h-mìhng seuhngmihn góng mātyéh.
I was only doing... kilometers an hour.	我行嘅時速只係...公里。 Ngóh hàahng-gán ge sìhchūk jí haih ... gūngléih.

喺邊度發生㗎。	Where did it happen?
幾時發生㗎。	What time did it happen?
你唔見咗乜嘢?	What's missing?
俾人偷咗啲乜嘢?	What's been taken?
俾我睇吓你嘅身份証 / 護照。	Could I see your identity card/passport?
有冇証人呀?	Are there any witnesses?
唔該你喺 (呢) 度簽名。	Sign here, please.
你需唔需要個翻譯呀?	Do you want an interpreter?

I'll have my car checked.	我即刻去檢查我架車。
	Ngóh jīkhāk heui gímchàh ngóh ga chē.
I was blinded by oncoming lights.	迎面嘅車燈爍住我對眼。
	Yìhngmihn ge chēdāng chàahng-jyuh ngóh deui ngáahn.

At the police station

I want to report a collision.	我要報案，係撞車。
	Ngóh yiu bou'ngon, haih johng-chē.
I want to report a missing person.	我要報案，係失蹤。
	Ngóh yiu bou'ngon, haih sātjūng.
I want to report a rape	我要報案，係強姦。
	Ngóh yiu bou'ngon, haih kèuhnggāan.
Could you make a statement, please?	你可唔可以俾筆供呀?
	Néih hó-m̀h-hóyíh béi bātgūng a?
Could I have a copy for the insurance?	我可唔可以要一份副本呀?
	Ngóh hó-m̀h-hóyíh yiu yāt fahn fubún a?
I've lost everything.	我所有嘅嘢都唔見咗喇。
	Ngóh sóyáuh ge yéh dōu m̀h'gin-jó la.
I've no money left, I'm desperate.	我嘅錢都用完喇，我走頭無路喇。
	Ngóh ge chín* dōu yuhng-yùhn la, ngóh jáutàuh mòuh-louh la.
Could you lend me a little money?	你可唔可以借啲錢俾我呀?
	Néih hó-m̀h-hóyíh je dī chín* béi ngóh a?
I'd like an interpreter.	我需要個翻譯。
	Ngóh sēuiyiu go fāanyihk.
I'm innocent.	我係無辜㗎。
	Ngóh haih mòuhgū ga.
I don't know anything about it.	我乜嘢都唔知道。
	Ngóh mātyéh dōu m̀h'jīdou.
I want to speak to someone from the American embassy.	我要同美國大使館嘅人講嘢。
	Ngóh yiu tùhng Méihgwo Daaihsíh-gwún ge yàhn góng-yéh.
I want a lawyer who speaks...	我要搵個會講 ... 嘅律師。
	Ngóh yiu wán go wúih góng ... ge leuhtsī.

15

Word list

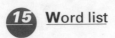

15 Word list

Word list English–Cantonese

The following word list is meant to supplement the chapters in this book.

Some of the words not contained in this list can be found elsewhere in the book, eg. alongside the diagrams of the car and bicycle.

A

abacus	syunpùhn	算盤
about (approximately)	daaihyeuk	大約
about (regarding)	yáuh'gwāan	有關
above	seuhngmihn	上面
abroad	gwok'ngoih	國外
accident	yi'ngoih	意外
accommodation	jyuhsūk	住宿
activity	wuhtduhng	活動
address	deihjí	地址
adult	sìhngyàhn	成人
advice	yigin	意見
aeroplane	fēigēi	飛機
afraid	pa	怕
after	jīhauh	之後
afternoon (midday)	jūng'nģh	中午
afternoon (3 pm to dusk)	hah'nģh	下午
again	joi	再
ago	yíhchìhn	以前
agree, to	tùhngyi	同意
air	hūnghei	空氣
air conditioning	hūngtiuh	空調
airmail	hòhnghūng-yàauhgín*	航空郵件
airplane	fēigēi	飛機
airport	fēigēi-chèuhng	飛機場
alcohol, liquor	jáu	酒
alike	sēungchíh	相似
a lot	hóudō	好多
almost	gēifùh	幾乎
alone	dāanduhk	單獨
alphabet	jihmóuh	字母
already	yíhgīng	已經
also	dōu	都
altogether, in total	yātguhng	一共
always	gīngsèuhng	經常
ambassador	daaihsíh	大使
America	Méihgwok	美國
American (in general)	Méihgwok ge	美國嘅
American (people)	Méihgwok-yàhn	美國人
amount	soumuhk	數目
ancestor	jóusīn	祖先
ancient	gúdoih	古代
and	tùhngmàaih	同埋
angry	faat'nāu/lāu	發嬲
animal	duhngmaht	動物
another (different)	daihyih go	第二個
another (same again)	joi làih yāt go	再嚟一個

answer the phone	jip-dihnwá*	接電話
anybody, anyone	yahmhòh-yàhn	任何人
apartment	gūngyuh	公寓
apologize, to	douhhip	道歉
apple	pìhnggwó	蘋果
appointment	yeuk`wuih/yuhyeuk	約會／預約
April	Sei-yuht	四月
architecture	ginjūk	建築
area	deihkēui	地區
around (nearby)	fuhgahn	附近
arrive, to	dou	到
Asia	Ngajāu	亞洲
ask about, to	mahn	問
ask for, to	yiu	要
asleep	fan-jeuhk	瞓着
assist, to	bōngjoh/bōngmòhng	幫助／幫忙
as well	dōu haih	都係
at	hái/héung	喺／響
at home	hái/héung ngūk/ūk`kéi	喺／響…屋企
at least	héimáh/jisíu	起碼／至少
at night	yehmáahn	夜晚
at once	jīkhāk	即刻
at the latest	jeuichìh	最遲
attempt, to	si	試
attend, to	chāamga	參加
attitude	taaidouh	態度
August	Baat-yuht	八月
Australia	Ngoujāu	澳洲
Australian (people)	Ngoujāu- yàhn	澳洲人
Australian (in general)	Ngoujāu ge	澳洲嘅
automobile, car	chē	車
autumn	chāutīn	秋天
available	máaih-dāk-dóu*	買得到
(can be purchased)		
available, to make	jéunbeih-hou	準備好
average (numbers)	pìhnggwān	平均
average (so-so, just okay)	yātbun/màh`má*-déi*	一般／麻麻地
awake	séng	醒
awake, wake up	séng*-jó	醒咗
awaken, wake someone up	giu-séng*	叫醒
aware	jīdou	知道

B

baby	bìhbī	BB
back, rear	hauhmihn	後面
back, to go	fāan-heui	返去
backward	lohkhauh	落後
bad	waaih	壞
bad luck	m̀h`hóuwahn/dóumùih	唔好運／倒霉
bag	dói*	袋
baggage	hàhngléih	行李
ball	bō	波
ballpoint pen	yùhnjí-bāt	原子筆
banana	hēungjīu	香蕉
bandage	bāngdáai*	繃帶
bank (finance)	ngàhnhòhng	銀行
banquet	yinwuih	宴會
bar (serving drinks)	jáubā	酒巴
barber	faatyìhng-sī	髮型師

bargain, to	góngga	講價
basket	láam*	籃
basketball	làahmkàuh	籃球
bathtub	yuhkgōng	浴缸
bathe, take a bath	chūnglèuhng	沖涼
bathe, swim	yàuhséui	游水
bathrobe	yuhkyī	浴衣
bathroom	chūnglèuhng-fóng*	沖涼房
be, exist	yáuh	有
beach	hóitāan	海灘
beancurd	dauhfuh	豆腐
beautiful	leng/jeng	靚／正
(of things and places)		
because	yānwaih	因為
bed	chòhng	床
bedclothes	seuihyī	睡衣
bedroom	seuihfóng*	睡房
bedsheet	chòhngdāan	床單
beef	ngàuhyuhk	牛肉
before (in time)	yíhchìhn	以前
before (in front of)	hái/héung ... chìhnmihn	喺／響... 前面
beforehand, earlier	jīchìhn	之前
begin, to	hōichí	開始
behave	bíuyihn	表現
behind	hái/héung ... hauhmihn	喺／響... 後面
Beijing	Bākgīng	北京
belief, faith	seunyéuhng	信仰
believe, to	sēungseun	相信
below	hahmihn	下面
belt	pèihdáai*	皮帶
beside	hái/héung ... pòhngbīn	喺／響... 旁邊
besides	chèuih-jó ... jī`ngoih	除咗之外
best	jeuihóu	最好
best wishes	jūk néih hóuwahn	祝你好運
better	gang`hóu / hóu-dī	更好／好啲
between	hái/héung ... jīgāan	喺／響... 之間
bicycle	dāanchē	單車
big	daaih	大
bill	dāan	單
bill, to pay	màaih-dāan	埋單
bird	jéuk*	雀
birth, to give	sāang	生
birthday	sāangyaht	生日
biscuit	bénggōn	餅乾
bit (slightly)	yātdī	一啲
bite, to	ngáauh	咬
bitter	fú	苦
black	hāksīk	黑色
bland	dāandiuh	單調
blanket	jīn	氈
bleed, to	làuh-hyut	流血
blood	hyut	血
blouse	néuihjōng-sēutsāam	女裝恤衫
blue	làahm`sīk	藍色
board, to (bus, train)	séuhng-chē	上車
board, to (boat)	séuhng-syùhn	上船
boat	syùhn	船
body	sāntái	身體
boil, to	jyú	煮

boiled	jyú-gwo ge	煮過嘅
bon voyage!	yāt-fàahn-fūng-seuhn	一帆風順
book	syū	書
bored	muhn/mòuhlìuh	悶／無聊
boring	móuh yisī	冇意思
born, to be	chēutsai	出世
borrow, to	je	借
botanic gardens	jihkmaht-yúhn	植物園
both	léuhng (go)	兩（個）
bother, disturb	dágáau	打攪
bottle	jēun	樽
bottom (buttocks)	lōyáu/peigú	攞柚／屁股
bowl	wún	碗
box	sēung	箱
box (cardboard)	jí'háp*	紙盒
boy	nàahm/làahm'jái	男仔
boyfriend	nàahm-pàhngyáuh	男朋友
bra	yúhjaau	乳罩
bracelet	sáu'ngáak	手鈪
brain	nóuh	腦
brake, to brake	saat-jai	剎掣
branch (company)	fānhóng*	分行
brand name	mìhngpàaih	名牌
bread	mihnbāau	面包
break, shatter	da-laahn	打爛
break down, to (car, machine)	waaih-jó	壞咗
breakfast, morning meal	jóuchāan	早餐
breakfast, to eat	sihk-jóuchāan	食早餐
breasts	yúhfòhng	乳房
bridge	kìuh	橋
briefcase	gūngsih-bāau	公事包
bring, to	ló	攞
Britain	Yīnggwok	英國
British (in general)	Yīnggwok ge	英國嘅
British (people)	Yīnggwok-yàhn	英國人
broccoli	sāilàahnfā-choi	西蘭花菜
bronze	tùhng/chīngtùhng	銅／青銅
brother (older)	gòhgō/daaihlóu	哥哥／大佬
brother (younger)	dàihdái*/sailóu	弟弟／細佬
brown (coffee color)	jyūgūlīk-sīk	朱古力色
bruise	yúhāk	瘀黑
brush	cháat*	刷
Buddhism	Fahtgaau	佛教
Buddhist (in general)	Fahtgaau ge	佛教嘅
Buddhist (people)	Fahtgaau-tòuh	佛教徒
building	daaihhah	大廈
burn (injury)	sīu-sēung	燒傷
Burma	Míhndihn	緬甸
Burmese (in general)	Míhndihn ge	緬甸嘅
Burmese (people)	Míhndihn-yàhn	緬甸人
bus	bāsí	巴士
bus stop	bāsí-jaahm	巴士站
business	sēungyihp	商業
businessperson	sēungyàhn	商人
busy (doing something)	mòhng	忙
but	daahnhaih	但係
butter	ngàuh/àuh'yàuh	牛油
buttocks	peigú/lōyáu	屁股／攞柚

| buy, to | máaih | 買 |
| by means of | yuhng | 用 |

c

cabbage	yèhchoi	野菜
cabbage, Chinese	baakchoi	白菜
cake, pastry	daahn'gōu	蛋糕
calculator	gaisou-gēi	計數機
call on the telephone	dá-dihnwá*	打電話
called, named	giujouh	叫做
Cambodia	Gōumìhn/Gáanpòuhjaaih	高棉／柬埔寨
Cambodian (in general)	Gōumìhn ge /	高棉嘅／
	Gáanpòuhjaaih ge	柬埔寨嘅
Cambodian (people)	Gōumìhn-yàhn/	高棉人／
	Gáanpòuhjaaih-yàhn	柬埔寨人
camera	yíngséung*-gēi	影相機
can, be able to	wúih	會
can, may	hóyíh	可以
can, tin	gwuntáu*	罐頭
cancel	chéuisīu	取消
candle	laahpjūk	蠟燭
candy, sweets	tóng*	糖
can't see	tái-m̀h'gin	睇唔見
can't see clearly	tái-m̀h'chīngchó	睇唔清楚
Cantonese (in general)	Gwóngdūng ge	廣東嘅
Cantonese (language)	Gwóngdūng-wá*	廣東話
Cantonese (people)	Gwóngdūng-yàhn	廣東人
capture, to	jūk-dóu*	捉到
car, automobile	chē	車
care of, to take	jiugu	照顧
careful!	síusām	小心
carrot	hùhng-lòhbaahk	紅蘿蔔
carry, to	daai/ló	帶／攞
cash, money	yihnfún	現款
cash a check, to	deuiyihn	兌現
cassette	hahp'sīk-luhkyām-dáai*	盒式錄音帶
cat	māau	貓
catch, to	jūk	捉
Catholic (in general)	Tīnjyúgaau ge	天主教嘅
Catholic (people)	Tīnjyúgaau-tòuh	天主教徒
cauliflower	yèhchoi-fā	椰菜花
cautious	síusām	小心
cave	ngàahmduhng	岩洞
CD (compact disc)	(gwōng)díp*	（光）碟
celebrate, to	hingjūk	慶祝
center, middle	jūnggāan	中間
certain, sure	yātdihng	一定
chair	dang	凳
chance, opportunity	gēiwuih	機會
change, small	sáan'ngán*	散銀
change, to (conditions, situations)	góibin	改變
change, switch (clothes)	wuhn	換
cheap	pèhng	平
cheat, to	ngāk/āk(yàhn)	呃（人）
check, verify	gímchàh	檢查
cheers!	yámsing	飲勝
cheese	jīsí	芝士
chess	gwokjai-jeuhngkéi*	國際象棋

chest (breast)	hūng	胸
chicken	gāi	雞
child (young person)	saimānjái	細蚊仔
child (offspring)	jái'néui*	仔女
chilli pepper	laahtjīu	辣椒
chilli sauce	laahtjīu-jeung	辣椒醬
China	Jūnggwok	中國
Chinese (in general)	Jūnggwok ge	中國嘅
Chinese (language)	Jūngmán*/Jūngmàhn	中文
Chinese (people)	Jūnggwok-yàhn	中國人
Chinese chess	jeuhngkéi*	象棋
chocolate	jyūgūlīk	朱古力
choice, to choose	syúnjaahk	選擇
chopsticks	faaijí	筷子
Christian	Gēidūk-tòuh	基督徒
Christianity	Gēidūk-gaau	基督教
church	gaau'tòhng/tóng*	教堂
cigarette	yīnjái	煙仔
cinema	heiyún	戲院
circle	yùhn'hyūn	圓圈
citizen	síhmàhn/gūngmàhn	市民／公民
city	sìhngsíh	城市
clean	gōnjehng	乾淨
clean, to	jíng-gōnjehng	整乾淨
clear (of weather)	hóutīn	好天
clever	chūngmìhng	聰明
climate	heihauh	氣候
clock	jūng	鐘
close to, nearby	káhn/kaaugahn	近／靠近
close, to cover	kám-màaih	冚埋
closed (door/shop)	sāan-mùhn	門門
closed (road)	fūngsó-jó	封鎖咗
clothes, clothing	yīfuhk	衣服
cloudy, overcast	dōwàhn	多雲
coat, jacket	ngoihyī	外衣
coat, overcoat	daaihlāu	大褸
coffee	gafē	咖啡
coin	ngán*jái／sáan'ngán*	銀仔／散銀
cold	dung	凍
cold, flu	sēungfūng	傷風
colleague, co-worker	tùhngsih	同事
collect payment, to	sāu-chín*	收錢
collision, to collide	johng	撞
colour	ngàahnsīk	顏色
comb	sō	梳
come, to	làih	嚟
come back	fāan-làih	返嚟
come in	yahp-làih	入嚟
comfortable	syūfuhk	舒服
company, firm	gūngsī	公司
compared with, to compare	béigaau	比較
complain, to	póuh'yun	抱怨
complaint	tàuhsou	投訴
complete (whole)	chyùhnbouh	全部
complete, to	yùhnsìhng	完成
complicated	fūkjaahp	複雜
computer	dihnnóuh	電腦
concert	yām'ngohk-wúi*	音樂會
concert hall	yām'ngohk-tēng	音樂廳

condom	beihyahn-tou	避孕套
confirm	kokyihng	確認
Confucianism	Yùhgā-sīséung	儒家思想
congratulations!	gūnghéi néih	恭喜你
consider (to think over)	háauleuih	考慮
consulate	líhngsih-gwún	領事館
consultation (by doctor)	tái-behng	睇病
contact, connection	lyùhnlok	聯絡
contact lens	yányìhng-ngáahn'géng*	隱型眼鏡
contagious	chyùhn'yíhm	傳染
continue, to	gaijuhk	繼續
contraceptive	beihyahn	避孕
contraceptive pill	beihyahn-yún	避孕丸
convenient	fōngbihn	方便
cook (person)	chyùhsī	廚師
cookie, sweet biscuit	kūkkèih	曲奇
cool (temperature)	lèuhngsóng	涼爽
copper	tùhng/jítùhng	銅／紫銅
copy	fubún	副本
corn, grain	sūkmáih	粟米
corner	goklōktáu*	角落頭
correct	ngāam/jingkok	啱／正確
correspond (write letters)	tūngseun	通信
corrupt	fuhbaaih	腐敗
cosmetics	fajōng-bán	化妝品
cost	sìhngbún	成本
cost (price)	gachìhn	價錢
costly	gwai	貴
cotton	mìhnbou	棉布
cotton wool	mìhnfā	棉花
couch, sofa	sōfá*	梳化
cough, to	kāt	咳
cough lolly	yeuhnhàuh-tóng*	潤喉糖
cough syrup	kāt-yeuhkséui	咳藥水
could, might	hó'nàhng	可能
count	sóu*	數
country (nation)	gwokgā	國家
courtesy	láihmaauh	禮貌
cover, to	jē	遮
crab	háaih	蟹
cracker, salty biscuit	hàahm-bénggōn	鹹餅乾
crafts	sáugūng-ngaih	手工藝
crashed (car)	johng-chē	撞車
credit card	seunyuhng-kāat	信用卡
cross, go over	gwo	過
crossroads	sahpjih-louhháu	十字路口
crowded	bīk	逼
cucumber	wòhnggwā	黃瓜
culture	màhnfa	文化
cup	būi	杯
custom, tradition	jaahpjuhk	習俗
cut, to	chit/got	切／割
cute, appealing	hó'ngoi	可愛

D

daily	yahtsèuhng	日常
damage, to	jíng'waaih	整壞
damp	chìuhsāp	潮濕
dance, to	tiumóuh	跳舞

danger, dangerous	ngàihhím	危險
dark	ngam	暗
date (of the month)	yahtkèih	日期
date of birth	chēutsāng yahtkèih	出生日期
daughter	néui*	女
day	yaht	日
day after tomorrow	hauhyaht	後日
day before yesterday	chìhnyaht	前日
dead	séi-jó	死咗
December	Sahp-yih-yuht	十二月
decision, to decide	kyutdihng	決定
deep	sām	深
defecate, to	daaihbihn	大便
degrees (temperature)	douh	度
delay, to	dāam'ngh	耽誤
delicious	hóusihk	好食
depart, to	lèihhōi	離開
department store	baakfo-gūngsī	百貨公司
departure	chēutfaat	出發
desk	syū'tói	書檯
dessert	tìhmbán	甜品
destination	muhkdīk-deih	目的地
detergent	sáigit-jīng	洗潔精
dial, to (telephone)	dá-dihnwá*	打電話
diamond	jyunchk	鑽石
diary	yahtgei	日記
dictionary	chìhdín/jihdín	詞典／字典
die, to	séi	死
different, other	m̀h'tùhng	唔同
difficult	kwan'nàahn	困難
dinner, evening meal	máahntaahn	晚飯
dinner, to eat	sihk-máahnfaahn	食晚飯
direction	fōngheung	方向
dirty	wūjōu	污糟
disappointed	sātmohng	失望
discount	gáam-ga	減價
dish, platter	dihp	碟
dish (particular food)	sung	餸
distance	kéuihlèih	距離
disturb, to	dágáau	打攪
divorce, to	lèih-fan	離婚
divorced	lèih-jó-fān	離咗婚
do, perform an action	jouh	做
don't mention it!	m̀h'hóu haakhei	唔好客氣
do one's best	jeuhn só'nàhng	盡所能
doctor	yīsāng	醫生
dog	gáu	狗
door	mùhn	門
double	sēungpúih	雙倍
down, downward	heunghah	向下
downstairs	làuhhah	樓下
downtown	síh-jūngsām	市中心
dozen	(yāt) dā	（一）打
draw, to	waahk	畫
drawer	gwaihtúng	櫃桶
dream	muhng	夢
dream, to	faat-muhng	發夢
dressed, to get	wuhn-sāam	換衫
dressing gown	sàhnlāu	晨褸

drink, refreshment	yámyéh	飲嘢
drink, to	yám	飲
drive, to (a car)	hōi-chē	開車
drug (medicine)	yeuhk	藥
drugstore, pharmacy	yeuhkfòhng	藥房
drunk	yám-jeui	飲醉
dry	gōn	乾
dry (weather)	gōnchou	乾燥
dry, to	chēui-gōn	吹乾
duck	ngaap/aap	鴨
during	hái/héung .... kèihgāan	喺 / 響...期間

E

ear	yíhjái	耳仔
earrings	yíhwáan	耳環
early	jóu	早
early in the morning	jiujóu	朝早
east	dūng'bīn/bihn	東邊
easy	yùhngyih	容易
eat, to	sihk	食
eat breakfast	sihk-jóuchāan	食早餐
eat dinner	sihk-máahnfaahn	食晚飯
eat lunch	sihk-ngaanjau	食晏晝
egg	gāidáan*	雞蛋
eggplant, aubergine	ngái'gwā	矮瓜
eight	baat	八
eighteen	sahp-baat	十八
eighty	baat-sahp	八十
either	yāthaih ... yāthaih	一係... 一係
elegant	gōu'ngáh	高雅
elevator	dihntāi	電梯
eleven	sahp-yāt	十一
embassy	daaihsíh-gwún	大使館
embroidered	saufā ge	繡花嘅
embroidery	chisau	刺繡
emergency	gāpchán	急診
empty	hūng ge	空嘅
engaged (telephone)	yáuh yàhn góng-gán	有人講緊
engaged (to be married)	dihng-fān	訂婚
England	Yīnggwok	英國
English (in general)	Yīnggwok ge	英國嘅
English (language)	Yīngmán* / Yīngmàhn/Yīngyúh	英文 / 英語
English (person)	Yīnggwok-yàhn	英國人
enlarge, to	fong-daaih	放大
enough	jūkgau	足夠
enquire, to	mahn	問
enter, to	yahp-làih	入嚟
entrance, way in	yahp'háu	入口
envelope	seunfūng	信封
envious, envy	sihnmouh	羨慕
environment, the	wàahn'gíng	環境
escalator	dihnduhng-làuhtāi	電動樓梯
Europe	Ngāujāu	歐洲
evening	yehmáahn	夜晚
everybody, everyone	múih go yàhn	每個人
every kind of	gok-sīk gok-yeuhng	各式各樣
everything	yatchai	一切
every time	múih chi	每次

everywhere	dou'chyu	到處
exact, exactly	koksaht	確實
exam, test	háau-síh	考試
examine, to	gímchàh	檢查
exchange, to (money, opinions)	deuiwuhn	兌換
exchange rate	deuiwuhn-léut*	兌換率
excited	gám-dou hīngfáhn	感到興奮
exciting	lihng yàhn hīngfáhn	令人興奮
excuse me! (attracting attention)	chéng/chíng'mahn	請問
excuse me! (getting past)	m̀h'gōi jeje	唔該借借
excuse me! (apology)	deui'm̀h-jyuh	對唔住
exit, way out	chēutháu	出口
expenses	faiyuhng	費用
expensive	gwai	貴
explain, to	gáaisīk	解釋
export, to export	chēutháu	出口
eye	ngáahn	眼
eyeglasses, spectacles	ngáahn'géng*	眼鏡

F

fabric, textile	bouliú*	布料
face	mihn	臉
face (respect)	mihnjí	面子
fall (season)	chāutīn	秋天
fall, to	dit	跌
fall over	dit-dóu	跌倒
false (imitation)	mouhpàaih-fo/gá'mouh ge	冒牌貨／假冒嘅
family	gātìhng	家庭
famous	yáuhméng*/chēutméng*	有名／出名
far	yúhn	遠
fast, rapid	faai	快
fatty, greasy	fèihneih/yàuh'neih	肥膩／油膩
father	bàhbā	爸爸
fax, to fax	chyùhnjān	傳真
fear	pa	怕
February	Yih-yuht	二月
fee	sāufai	收費
feel, to	gokdāk	覺得
female	néuihsing	女性
festival	jityaht	節日
fetch, to	ló	攞
fever	faatsīu	發燒
few	géi go	幾個
fifteen	sahp-ńgh	十五
fifty	ńgh-sahp	五十
Filipino (Tagalog)	Fēileuhtbān-yúh	菲律賓語
fill out (form)	tìhn-bíu	填表
film (camera)	fēilám*	菲林
film, movie	dihnyíng	電影
find, to	wán	搵
finger	sáují	手指
fire	fó	火
fireworks	yīnfā	煙花
first, earlier, beforehand	sīn	先
fish	yú*	魚
fish, to	diu-yú*	釣魚
fitting room	sisān-sāt	試身室

five	ngh	五
flash (camera)	sím'gwōng-dāng	閃光燈
flashlight, torch	dihntúng	電筒
flavour	meihdouh	味道
flight	bāan'gēi	班機
flight number	bāan'gēi-houh	班機號
floor	láu*	樓
flower	fā	花
fly (insect)	wūyīng	烏蠅
flu	gámmouh	感冒
fog	mouh	霧
follow along, to	seuhn-jyuh	順住
follow behind, to	gān-jyuh	跟住
fond of, to be	jūngyi/héifūn	鐘意／喜歡
food	sihkmaht	食物
foot	geuk	腳
forbid, to	gamjí	禁止
foreign	ngoihgwok ge	外國嘅
foreigner	ngoihgwok-yàhn	外國人
forget, to	mòhnggei	忘記
fork	chā	叉
fortunately	hóuchói	好彩
forty	sei-sahp	四十
forward	heungchìhn	向前
four	sei	四
fourteen	sahp-sei	十四
France	Faatgwok	法國
French (in general)	Faatgwok ge	法國嘅
French (language)	Faatmán*/Faatmàhn	法文
French (people)	Faatgwok-yàhn	法國人
free, independent	jihyàuh	自由
free of charge	míhnfai	免費
frequent	gīngsèuhng	經常
fresh	sānsīn	新鮮
Friday	Sīngkèih-ngh/Láihbaai-ngh	星期五／禮拜五
friend	pàhngyáuh	朋友
friendly, outgoing	yáuhsihn	友善
front	chìhnmihn	前面
fruit	sāanggwó	生果
fry, to	jīn	煎
full, eaten one's fill	báau	飽
fun, to have	wáan	玩
funny	hóusiu	好笑
future: in future	jēunglòih	將來

G

gamble	dóubok	賭博
game	yàuhhei	遊戲
garage (for repairs)	jíngchē-chóng	整車廠
garbage	laahpsaap	垃圾／
gardens, park	gūngyún	公園
garlic	syuntàuh	蒜頭
garment	yīfuhk	衣服
gasoline	dihnyàuh	電油
gasoline station	dihnyàuh-jaahm	電油站
German (in general)	Dākgwok ge	德國嘅
German (language)	Dākmán*/Dākmàhn	德文
German (people)	Dākgwok-yàhn	德國人
Germany	Dākgwok	德國

get off (bus/train)	lohk-chē	落車
get off (boat)	lohk-syùhn	落船
get on (bus/train)	séuhng-chē	上車
get on (boat)	séuhng-syùhn	上船
get up (from bed)	héisān	起身
gift	láihmaht	禮物
girlfriend	néuih-pàhngyáuh	女朋友
give, to	béi	俾
given name	méng*	名
glad	gōuhing	高興
glass (for drinking)	bōlēi-būi	玻璃杯
glasses, spectacles	ngáahn'géng*	眼鏡
go, to	heui	去
go around, visit	fóngmahn	訪問
go home	fāan-ngūkkéi*	返屋企
go out, exit	chēut-heui	出去
go to bed	fan'gaau	瞓覺
gold	gām	金
golf	gōuyíhfū-kàuh	高爾夫球
good	hóu	好
goodbye	joigin	再見
good luck!	jūk néih hóuwahn	祝你好運
grapes	(pòuh) tàihjí	(葡) 提子
green	luhksīk	綠色
grow, cultivate	jung	種
Guangzhou (Canton)	Gwóngjāu	廣州
guide, lead	douhyàuh	導遊
guidebook	léuihyàuh-jí'nàahm	旅遊指南

H

hair	tàuhfaat	頭髮
half	yatbun	一半
hand	sáu	手
handicraft	sáugūng'ngaih	手工藝
handsome	yīngjeun	英俊
happen, occur	faatsāng	發生
happy	hoisam/gouhing	開心 / 高興
Happy Birthday!	Sāangyaht Faailohk	生日快樂
Happy Chinese New Year!	Gūnghéi Faatchòih	恭喜發財
harbor	hóigóng	海港
hardworking, industrious	kàhnlihk	勤力
harmonious	yùhnghāp	融洽
have, own	yáuh	有
have to, must	yātdihng yiu	一定要
he, him	kéuih	佢
head	tàuh	頭
headache	tàuhtung	頭痛
healthy	gihnhōng	健康
hear, to	tēng	聽
heart	sāmjohng	心臟
heavy	chúhng	重
hello, hi	néih hóu	你好!
hello! (on phone)	wái	喂
Help!	Gau'mehng a!	救命啊!
help, to	bōng/bōngmòhng	幫 / 幫忙
her, hers	kéuih ge	佢嘅
here	nīdouh / nīsyu	呢度 / 呢處
high	gōu	高
hill	sāan	山

hire, to	jōu	租
his	kéuih ge	佢嘅
history	lihksí	歷史
hit, strike	dá	打
hobby	ngoi'hou	愛好
holiday (festival)	jityaht	節日
holiday (vacation)	gakèih	假期
home, house	ngūkkéi*/ūkkéi*	屋企
honest	sìhngsaht	誠實
honey	mahttòhng	蜜糖
Hong Kong	Hēunggóng	香港
hope, to	hēi'mohng	希望
horse	máh	馬
hospital	yīyún	醫院
hot (spicy)	laaht	辣
hot (temperature)	yiht	熱
hotel	léuihgwún	旅館
hot spring	wānchyùhn	溫泉
hour	jūngtàuh	鐘頭
how?	dím/yùhhòh	點 / 如何
how are you?	néih hóu ma	你好嗎
however	daahnhaih	但係
how far?	Géi yúhn?	幾遠?
how long?	Géi chèuhng?	幾長?
how many?	Géi go?	幾個?
how much?	Géidō chín*?	幾多錢?
how old?	Géi daaih nìhn'géi?	幾大年紀?
humid	chìuhsāp	潮濕
humor	yāumahk	幽默
hundred	baak	百
hundred thousand	sahp-maahn	十萬
hundred million	yīk	億
hungry	ngoh	餓
hurry up!	faai-dī	快啲
hurt (injured)	sauhsēung	受傷
husband	jeuhngfū	丈夫

I

I, me	ngóh	我
ice	bīng	冰
ice cream	syutgōu	雪糕
idea	jyúyi	主意
if	yùh'gwó	如果
illegal	fēifaat	非法
ill, sick	m̀h'syūfuhk	唔舒服
illness	behng	病
immediately	laahp'hāk	立刻
impolite	móuh-láihmaauh	冇禮貌
important	juhngyiu	重要
impossible	móuh hó'nàhng	冇可能
in, at (space)	hái/héung ... yahpbihn	喺 / 響 ...入邊
in (time, years)	hái/héung ... hauh	喺 / 響 ...後
included, including	bāau'kwut	包括
increase, to increase	jānggā	增加
indigenous (in general)	tóujyu ge	土著嘅
indigenous (people)	tóujyu	土著
India	Yandouh	印度
Indian	Yandouh ge	印度嘅
Indian	Yandouh-yàhn	印度人

Indonesia	Yan'nèih/Yandouhnèihsāi'a	印尼 / 印度尼西亞
Indonesian (in general)	Yan'nèih ge	印尼嘅
Indonesian (language)	Yan'nèih-yúh	印尼語
Indonesian (people)	Yan'nèih-yàhn	印尼人
inexpensive	pèhng	平
influence, to	yínghéung	影響
inform, to	tūngjī	通知
information	seunsīk	信息
information desk	sēunmahn-chyu	詢問處
injection	dá-jām	打針
insect	chùhng	蟲
inside	léuihmihn/yahpbihn	裡面 / 入邊
inside of	hái/héung ... yahpbihn	喺 / 響 ... 入邊
inspect, to	gímchàh	檢查
insurance	bóuhím	保險
intend, to	dásyun	打算
interested in	gám hingcheui	感興趣
international	gwokjai	國際
interpreter	fāanyihk	翻譯
intersection	sahpjih-louhháu	十字路口
introduce someone, to	gaaisiuh	介紹
invitation, to invite	yiuching	邀請
Ireland	Ngoiyíhlàahn	愛爾蘭
Irish (in general)	Ngoiyíhlàahn ge	愛爾蘭嘅
Irish	Ngoiyíhlàahn- yàhn	愛爾蘭人
iron (metal)	tit	鐵
iron (for clothing)	tongdáu	熨斗
Islam	Yīsīlàahn'gaau / Wùihgaau	伊斯蘭教 / 回教
island	dóu	島
Italian (in general)	Yidaaihleih ge	意大利嘅
Italian (language)	Yidaaihleih'mán*/màhn	意大利文
Italian (people)	Yidaaihleih-yàhn	意大利人
Italy	Yidaaihleih	意大利
ivory	jeuhng'ngàh	象牙

J

jacket	ngoihtou	外套
jam	gwójeung	果醬
January	Yāt-yuht	一月
Japan	Yahtbún	日本
Japanese (in general)	Yahtbún ge	日本嘅
Japanese (language)	Yaht'mán*/màhn	日文
Japanese (people)	Yahtbún-yàhn	日本人
jewelry	sáusīk	手飾
job	gūngjok	工作
join, go along	chāamgā	參加
joke	siuwá*	笑話
joke, to	góngsiu	講笑
journey	louhchìhng	路程
juice	gwójāp	果汁
July	Chāt-yuht	七月
jump, to	tiu	跳
June	Luhk-yuht	六月
just, fair	gūngpìhng	公平
just now	ngāam'ngāam/āam'āam	啱啱

K

keep, to	bóulàuh	保留

key (to room)	sósìh	鎖匙
kilogram	gūnggān	公斤
kilometre	gūngléih	公里
kind, good (of persons)	hóusām	好心
kind, type	júngleuih	種類
kitchen	chyùhfóng*/chèuihfóng*	廚房
knee	sāttàuhgō	膝頭哥
knife	dōu	刀
know, be acquainted with	sīk	識
know, be informed	jīdou	知道
Korea, North	Bākhòhn/Chìuhsīn	北韓 / 朝鮮
Korea, South	Nàahmhòhn/Hòhn'gwok	南韓 / 韓國
Korean (North)	Chìuhsīn-yàhn	朝鮮人
Korean (South)	Hòhn'gwok-yàhn	韓國人
Korean (language)	Hòhnyúh/Chìuhsīnyúh,	韓語 / 朝鮮語
	Hòhnmàhn/Chìuhsīnmàhn	韓文 / 朝鮮文

L

lady	néuihsih	女士
lake	wùh	湖
lamb, mutton	yèuhng'yuhk	羊肉
lane (of a highway)	chēdouh/chēsin	車道 / 車線
language	yìhnyúh	言語
Laos	Lìuhgwok	寮國
Laotian	Lìuhgwok-yàhn	寮國人
large	daaih	大
last (final)	jeuihauh	最後
last (endure)	yìhnjuhk	延續
last night	kàhm/chàhm'máahn	琴 / 尋晚
last week	seuhng (go) sīngkèih/	上（個）星期 /
	láihbaai	禮拜
last year	gauh'nín*	舊年
late (for an appointment)	chìhdou	遲到
later	gwo yātjahn'gāan	過一陣間
laugh, to	siu	笑
lawyer	leuhtsī	律師
lazy	láahndoh	懶惰
lead (tour guide)	douhyàuh	導遊
leaded petrol	hàhm'yùhn-dihnyàuh	含鉛電油
learn, to	hohk	學
least (smallest amount)	jeuisíu	最少
least: at least	jisíu	至少
leather	péi*	皮
leave, depart	lèihhōi	離開
left-hand side	jó'bīn/bihn	左邊
leg	téui	腿
legal	hahpfaat	合法
lend, to	je	借
lessen, reduce	gáamsíu	減少
let someone know, to	wah béi ... jī	話俾 ... 知
letter	seun	信
level (height)	gōudouh	高度
level (standard)	bīujéun	標準
library	tòuhsyū-gwún	圖書館
license (for driving)	gasái-jāpjiu	駕駛執照
lie, tell a falsehood	góng-daaihwah	講大話
lift, elevator	dihntāi	電梯
light (not heavy)	hēng	輕
light (bright)	gwōng	光

light (lamp)	dāng	燈
lighter	dáhfóh-gēi	打火機
like, as	hóuchíh	好似
line up, to	pàaih-déui*	排隊
listen, to	tēng	聽
little (not much)	yātdī	一啲
little (small)	sai	細
live (stay in a place)	jyuh	住
lock, to	só	鎖
long (time)	noih	耐
long (size)	chèuhng	長
look at, see	tái	睇
look for	wán	搵
look out!	tái-jyuh	睇住
look up (find in book)	chàh	查
lose, be defeated	syū	輸
lose weight, to	gáam-bóng*/gáam-fèih	減磅 / 減肥
loud	daaihsēng	大聲
love	ngoi/oi`chìhng	愛情
love, to	ngoi/oi	愛
lovely	hó`ngoi/oi	可愛
lucky	hahng`wahn	幸運
luggage	hàhngléih	行李
lunch, midday meal	ńgh`chāan / ngaanjau	午餐 / 晏晝
lychee	laihjī	荔枝

M

Macau	Ngoumún*	澳門
madam (term of address)	taaitáai*	太太
magazine	jaahpji	雜誌
mahjong	mahjeuk	麻雀
mail, to	gei	寄
major (important)	juhngyiu	重要
make, to	jouh	做
Malaysia	Máhlòihsäi`nga	馬來西亞
Malaysian (in general)	Máhlòihsäi`nga ge	馬來西亞嘅
Malaysian (people)	Máhlòihsäi`nga-yàhn	馬來西亞人
male	nàahmsing	男性
man	nàahmyán*	男人
manager	gīngléih	經理
Mandarin (language)	Póutūng-wá*/Gwokyúh	普通話 / 國語
mango	mōnggwó	芒果
manners	láihmaauh	禮貌
manufacture, to	jaijouh	製造
many, much	hóudō	好多
map	deihtòuh	地圖
March	Sāam-yuht	三月
market	síhchèuhng	市場
marry, get married	git-fān	結婚
massage, to	ngonmō	按摩
match, game	béichoi	比賽
May	Ńgh-yuht	五月
maybe	waahkjé	或者
meaning	yisī	意思
measure, to	lèuhng	量
measurements	chekchyun/daaihsai	尺寸 / 大細
meat	yuhk	肉
medicine	yeuhk	藥
meet, to	ginmihn	見面

Word list

15

menstruate, to	làih-yuhtgīng	嚟月經
menu	choipáai*	菜牌
mess, in a	lyuhn-chāt-baat-jōu	亂七八糟
message	làuhyìhn	留言
meter	gūngchek	公尺
midday	ngaanjau/jūng'ngh	晏晝／中午
middle, centre	jūnggāan	中間
midnight	bunyeh	半夜
mild (not spicy)	chīngdaahm	清淡
mild (not cold)	wòh'nyúhn	和暖
milk	ngàuhnáaih	牛奶
millimeter	hòuhmáih	毫米
million	baak-maahn	百萬
mind, brain	nóuh	腦
mind, to be displeased	gaaiyi	介意
mineral water	kwongchyùhn-séui	礦泉水
mini	màih'néih	迷你
minute	fān (jūng)	分（鐘）
mirror	geng	鏡
Miss	síujé	小姐
miss, to	jáu-jó	走咗
(bus, flight etc.)	(bāsí, fēigēi)	（巴士，飛機）
miss, to (loved one)	gwa-jyuh	掛住
mistaken	gáau-cho	搞錯
misunderstanding	ngh'wuih	誤會
mobile phone	sáutàih-dihnwá*	手提電話
modern	yihndoih	現代
moment (in a moment)	dáng yātjahn	等一陣
Monday	Sīngkèih-yāt/Láihbaai-yāt	星期一／禮拜一
money	chín*	錢
month	yuht	月
moon	yuhtleuhng	月亮
more (comparative)	dō-dī	多啲
more of (things)	gang-dō	更多
more or less	daaihkoi	大概
moreover	yìhché	而且
morning	jiujóu	朝早
mosque	Wùihgaau-míu*	回教廟
mosquito	mān	蚊
most (superlative)	jeui	最
most (the most of)	jeuidō	最多
mostly	daaih-bouhfahn	大部分
mother	màhmā	媽媽
mother-in-law	ngoihmóu*	外母
motorcycle	dihndāanchē	電單車
motor vehicle	sīgā-chē	私家車
mountain	sāan	山
mouse (animal)	lóuhsyú	老鼠
mouth	jéui	嘴
move from one place to another	būn	搬
movement, motion	duhngjok	動作
movie	dihnyíng	電影
movie house	heiyún*	戲院
Mr	sīnsāang	先生
Mrs	taaitáai*	太太
MSG	meihjīng	味精
much, many	dō	多
muscle	gēiyuhk	肌肉

music	yām'ngohk	音樂
musical instrument	ngohkhei	樂器
museum	bokmaht-gwún	博物館
mushrooms	mòhgū/chógu	蘑菇 / 草菇
Muslim (in general)	Wùihgaau ge	回教嘅
Muslim (people)	Wùihgaau-tòuh	回教徒
must	yātdihng	一定
mutton	yèuhng'yuhk	羊肉
my, mine	ngóh ge	我嘅

N

nail (finger, toe)	jí'gaap	指甲
name	méng*	名
narrow	jaak	窄
nation, country	gwokgā	國家
national	chyùhn'gwok-sing	全國性
nationality	gwokjihk	國籍
natural	jihyìhn ge	自然嘅
nature	daaih-jihyìhn	大自然
naughty	wàahnpèih	頑皮
nearby	fuhgahn	附近
nearly	gēifùh	幾乎
neat, orderly	jíngchàih	整齊
necessary	bītsēui	必需
neck	géng	頸
necklace	génglín	頸鏈
necktie	léhnglāai	領吥
need, to need	sēuiyiu	需要
needle	jām	針
neither	léuhng go dōu m̀h'haih	兩個都唔係
never mind!	m̀h'gányiu	唔緊要
nevertheless	bātgwo	不過
new	sān	新
news	sanmán*/sānmàhn	新聞
newspaper	boují	報紙
New Zealand	Sānsāilàahn	新西蘭
New Zealander	Sānsāilàaln-yàhn	新西蘭人
next to	pòhngbīn	旁邊
next week	hah (go) sīngkèih/	下（個）星期 /
	láihbaai	禮拜
next year	mìhng/chēut'nín*	明年 / 出年
nice	hóu	好
night	yehmáahn(hāk)	夜晚(黑)
nightclothes, nightdress	seuihyī	睡衣
nine	gáu	九
nineteen	sahp-gáu	十九
ninety	gáu-sahp	九十
no, not have	móuh	冇
no, not	m̀h'haih	唔係
nobody	móuhyàhn	冇人
noise	sēng	聲
noisy	chòuh	嘈
noodles	mihn	麵
noon	jūng'ńgh	中午
normal	jingsèuhng	正常
north	bākbihn	北邊
north-east	dūngbāk	東北
north-west	sāibāk	西北
nose	beihgō	鼻哥

not	m̀h'haih	唔 / 唔係
not yet	juhng meih	仲未
note (written)	jihtìuh	字條
note down, to	gei-dāi	記低
nothing	móuhyéh	冇嘢
notice	tūngjī	通知
notice, to	jyuyi	注意
novel	síusyut	小説
November	Sahp-yāt-yuht	十一月
now	yìhgā	而家
nowadays	yìhnsìh	現時
nowhere	bīndouh dōu m̀h'hái	邊度都唔係
number	houhmáh	號碼

O

o'clock	dím(jūng)	點（鐘）
obedient	tēngwah	聽話
obey, to	fuhkchùhng	服從
object, thing	yéh	嘢
object, to protest	fáandeui	反對
occasionally	ngáuh'yìhn	偶然
occupation	jīkyihp	職業
ocean	hóiyèuhng	海洋
October	Sahp-yuht	十月
odor, bad smell	chau'hei	臭氣
of, from	(suhkyū) ... ge	（屬於）...嘅
of course	dōngyìhn	當然
off (gone bad)	waaih-jó	壞咗
off (turned off)	sāan-jó	閂咗
off: to turn something off	sāan	閂
offend	dākjeuih	得罪
offer, suggest	tàihyíh	提議
offering	tàihgūng	提供
office	séjih-làuh/baahn'gūng-sāt	寫字樓 / 辦公室
officials (government)	gūngmouh-yùhn	公務員
often	gīngsèuhng	經常
oil	yàuh	油
okay	dāk	得
old (of persons)	lóuh	老
old (of things)	gauh	舊
olden times, in	gauhsìh	舊時
Olympics	Ngouwahn-wúi*	奧運會
on, at	hái/héung	喺 / 響
on: to turn something on	hōi	開
on fire	fójūk	火燭
on foot	hàahnglouh heui	行路去
on the way	làih-gán	嚟緊
on the whole	daaihji-seuhng	大致上
on time	jéunsìh	準時
once	yāt chi	一次
one	yāt	一
one-way ticket	dāanchìhng-piu	單程票
onion	yèuhngchūng	洋蔥
only	jihnghaih	淨係
open	hōi	開
open, to	dá-hōi	打開
opinion	yigin	意見
opportunity	gēiwuih	機會
oppose, to	fáandeui	反對

15 Word list

opposite (facing)	deuimihn	對面
opposite (contrary)	sēungfáan	相反
or	waahkjé	或者
orange, citrus	cháang	橙
orange (colour)	cháangsīk	橙色
order (placed for food)	dím-choi	點菜
order, sequence	chijeuih	次序
organize, arrange	ngōnpàaih	安排
origin	héiyùhn	起源
original	jeuichō	最初
ornament	jōngsīk-bán	裝飾品
other	kèihtā	其他
other (alternative)	lihng'ngoih	另外
ought to	yīnggōi	應該
our	ngóh/óh'deih ge	我哋嘅
out	chēut-jó-gāai	出咗街
outside	ngoihmihn	外面
oval (shape)	tóh'yùhn-yìhng	橢圓形
overcast, cloudy	yāmtīn	陰天
overseas	hói'ngoih	海外
over there	gó'bīn/bihn	嗰邊
owe, to	him	欠
own, personal	jihgéi ge	自己嘅
oyster	hòuh	蠔

P

pack, to	baaujōng	包裝
paid	béi-jó-chín*	俾咗錢
pain, painful	tung	痛
painting	wá*	畫
pair of, a	yāt deui	一對
pajamas	seuihyī	睡衣
palace	wòhnggūng	宮殿
pan	wohk	鑊
panorama	chyùhn'gíng	全景
pants	fu	褲
paper	jí	紙
parcel	bāaugwó	包裹
pardon me?	mē wá*	咩話
what did you say?		
parents	fuhmóuh	父母
park	gūng'yún*	公園
park, to (car)	paak-chē	泊車
part (not whole)	bouhfahn	部分
participate, to	chāamgā	參加
particularly, especially	yàuhkèihsih	尤其是
partly	yāt bouhfahn	一部分
partner (in business)	paakdong	拍擋
partner (spouse)	buhnléuih	伴侶
pass, go past	gīnggwo	經過
pass, to (exam)	hahpgaak	合格
passenger	sìhnghaak	乘客
passport	wuhjiu	護照
past, former	gwoheui	過去
pastime	sīuhín	消遣
patient (calm)	noihsām	耐心
patient (doctor's)	behngyàhn	病人
pay, to	béi-chín*	俾錢
pay attention	làuhyi/juhyi	留意 / 注意

Word list

15

peach	tóu*	桃
peak, summit	sāandéng*	山頂
peanut	fāsāng	花生
pear	léi	梨
pearl	jānjyū	珍珠
pink	fánhùhng-sīk	粉紅色
pen	mahkséui-bāt	墨水筆
pencil	yùhnbāt	鉛筆
penis	yāmging	陰莖
people	yàhn	人
pepper (black)	hāk-wùhjīu-fán	黑胡椒粉
pepper (chilli)	laahtjīu	辣椒
percent	baakfahnjī…	百分之…
percentage	baakfahn-léut*	百分率
performance	yínchēut	演出
perfume	hēungséui	香水
perhaps	waahkjé	或者
perhaps, probably	hó'nàhng	可能
period (end of a sentence)	geuihouh	句號
period (of time)	sìhkèih	時期
permit	héuihó-jing	許可証
permit, to allow	jéunhéui	準許
person	yàhn	人
personality	singgaak	性格
perspire, to	chēut-hohn	出汗
pet animal	chúngmaht	寵物
petrol	dihnyàuh	電油
petrol station	dihnyàuh-jaahm	電油站
pharmacy, drugstore	yeuhkfòhng	藥房
Philippines	Fēileuhtbān	菲律賓
photocopy, to photocopy	fūkyan	複印
photograph	séung*	相
photograph, to	yíng-séung*	影相
pick, choose	gáan	揀
pick up, to (someone)	jip	接
pick up, lift (something)	jāp	執
pickpocket	pàhsáu	扒手
picture	wá*	畫
piece, item	gihn	件
pierce, penetrate	chyūn	穿
pig	jyū	猪
pills	yeuhk'yún	藥丸
pillow	jámtàuh	枕頭
pineapple	bōló	菠蘿
pink	fánhùhng-sīk	粉紅色
pity	hólìhn	可憐
pity: what a pity!	hósīk	可惜
place	deihfōng	地方
place, put	fong	放
plan, to	dásyun	打算
plane	fēigēi	飛機
plant	jihkmaht	植物
plant, to	jung	種
plastic	sokgāau	塑膠
plate	dihp	碟
play, to	wáan*	玩
please go ahead, please	chíng	請
pleased	gōuhing	高興
plug (bath)	sāk	塞

plug (electric)	chaap'táu*	插頭
plum	boulàm	布冧
pocket	dói*	袋
point out	jíchēut	指出
poisonous	yáuhduhk ge	有毒嘅
police	gíngchaat-gúk*	警察局
police officer	gíngchaat	警察
polite	yáuh-láihmaauh	有禮貌
poor (not rich)	kùhng	窮
popular	làuhhàhng	流行
population	yàhnháu	人口
pork	jyūyuhk	猪肉
port	hóigóng	海港
portion, serve	yāt fahn	一份
possess, to	yúngyáuh	擁有
possessions	chòihmaht	財物
possible, possibly	hó'nàhng	可能
post, mail	gei	寄
postcard	mìhngseun-pín*	明信片
post office	yàuhgúk*	郵局
postpone, to	yìhnkèih	延期
pour, to	dóu	倒
power	lihk	力
practice, to practice	lihnjaahp	練習
praise, to	jaan	讚
prawn	hā	蝦
prayer, to pray	kèihtóu	祈禱
prefer, to	jūngyi	鍾意
pregnant	wàaihyahn	懷孕
prepare, make ready	jéunbeih	準備
prepared, ready	jéunbeih-hóu	準備好
prescription	yeuhkdāan	藥單
present (here)	yìhgā	而家
present (gift)	láihmaht	禮物
presently, nowadays	gahnlòih	近來
present moment, at the	muhkchìhn	目前
pressure	ngaaklihk	壓力
pretend, to	jadai	咋帝
pretty	leng	靚
prevent, to	jójí	阻止
price	gachìhn	價錢
pride	jihhòuh , jihjyún-sām	自豪, 自專心
priest	sàhnfuh	神父
prison	gāamyuhk	監獄
private	sīyàhn	私人
probably	daaihkoi	大概
problem	mahntàih	問題
profession	jīkyihp	職業
program, schedule	jitmuhk	節目
promise, to	daapying	答應
pronounce, to	faatyām	發音
proof	jinggeui	証據
prove, to	jingmìhng	証明
public	gūngguhng	公共
pull, to	lāai	拉
pump	bāng	泵
punctual	jéunsìh	準時
pupil	hohksāang	學生
pure	sèuhn	純

purple	jísīk	紫色
purpose	muhkdīk	目的
purse (for money)	ngàhnbāau	銀包
push, to	tēui	推
put, place	fong	放
put off, delay	yìhnchìh	延遲
put on (clothes)	jeuk	著
pyjamas	seuihyī	睡衣

Q

qualification	jī'gaak	資格
quarter	seifahnjī-yāt	四分之一
question	mahntàih	問題
queue, line	chèuhnglùhng	長龍
queue, to line up	pàaih-déui*	排隊
quick	faai	快
quiet	ngōnjihng	安靜
quite (fairly)	sēungdōng	相當

R

radio	sāuyām-gēi	收音機
rail: by rail	chóh-fóchē	坐火車
railroad, railway	titlouh	鐵路
rain	yúh	雨
rain, to	lohk-yúh	落雨
raise, lift	tàihgōu	提高
raise, to (children)	fúyéuhng	撫養
rank, station in life	deihwaih	地位
rarely, seldom	nàahndāk	難得
rat	lóuhsyú	老鼠
rate, tariff	sāufai	收費
rate of exchange	deuiwuhn-léut*	兌換率
rather, fairly	béigaau	比較
rather than	nìhnghó	寧可
raw, uncooked, rare	sāang ge	生嘅
reach, get to	daahtdou	達到
reaction, response	fáanying	反應
read, to	tái-syū	睇書
ready	yìhnsìhng	現成
ready, to get	jéunbeih	準備
really (very)	fēisèuhng	非常
really?	haih mē?	係咩?
rear, tail	hauhmihn	後面
reason	yùhnyān	原因
reasonable (sensible)	hahpchìhng-hahp'léih	合情合理
reasonable (price)	gūngdouh	公道
receipt	sāugeui	收據
receive, to	sāu-dóu*	收到
recipe	sihkpóu	食譜
recognize, to	yìhngdāk	認得
recommend, to	tēuijin	推薦
recover (cured)	hōngfuhk	康復
rectangle	chèuhngfōng-yìhng	長方形
red	hùhngsīk	紅色
reduce, to	gáam-ga	減價
reduction	gáamsíu	減少
refrigerator	syut'gwaih	雪櫃
refusal, to refuse	kéuih'jyuht	拒絕
region	deihkēui	地區

register, to	gwahouh	掛號
registered post	gwahouh-seun	掛號信
relatives, family	chānchīk	親戚
relax, to	fongsūng	放鬆
religion	jūnggaau	宗教
remainder, leftover	jihng-lohk-làih ge	剩落嚟嘅
remains (historical)	gújīk	古迹
remember, to	geidāk	記得
remind, to	tàihséng	提醒
rent, to	jōu	租
repair, to	sāuléih	修理
repeat, to	chùhngfūk	重複
replace, to	doihtai	代替
reply, response	daapfūk	答覆
report	bougou	報告
reporter	geijé	記者
request, to	yīukàuh	要求
rescue, to	gau	救
research, to research	yìhn'gau	研究
resemble	chíh	似
reserve, to (ask for in advance)	yuhdehng	預訂
respect, to	jyūn'ging	尊敬
respond, react	fáanying	反應
response, reaction	daapfūk	答覆
responsibility	jaakyahm	責任
responsible, to be	fuhjaak	負責
rest, to relax	yāusīk	休息
restaurant	chāan'gwún	餐館
restroom	sáisáu-gāan	洗手間
result	sìhngjīk	成績
retired	teuiyāu	退休
return, to give back	wàahn	還
return, to go back	fāan-jyuntàuh	返轉頭
return ticket	lòihwùih-piu	來回票
reverse, to go back	diuhtàuh	掉頭
rice (cooked)	baahkfaahn	白飯
rice (uncooked grains)	máih	米
rich	fuyuh	富裕
ride (in car)	chóh-chē	坐車
ride, to (horse)	kèh-máh	騎馬
ride, to (bicyle)	cháai-dāanchē	踩單車
ride, to (motorcycle)	jā-dihndāanchē	揸電單車
right, correct	jingkok	正確
right-hand side	yauh'bīn/bihn	右邊
right now	laahp'hāk	立刻
ring (jewellery)	gaaijí	戒指
ring, to (on the telephone)	dá-dihnwá*	打電話
ring, to (bell)	gahm-jūng	撳鐘
rip open, to	sī-hōi	撕開
ripe	suhk ge	熟嘅
rise, increase	jānggā	增加
river	hòh	河
road	louh	路
rock	sehktàuh	石頭
room	fóng*	房
rotten	fuhlaahn	腐爛
roughly, approximately	daaihyeuk	大約
round (shape)	yùhnyìhng	圓形

round, around	wàahn'yíu	環繞
rude	móuh-láihmaauh	冇禮貌
rules	kwāijāk	規則

S

sad	nàahn'gwo	難過
safe	ngōnchyùhn	安全
salary	sānséui	薪水
sale, for	chēut'sauh	出售
sale (reduced prices)	daaih-gáamga	大減價
sales assistant	sauhfo-yùhn	售貨員
salt	yìhm	鹽
salty	hàahm	鹹
same	yātyeuhng	一樣
sample	yeuhngbún	樣本
sand	sā	沙
sandals	lèuhng'hàaih	涼鞋
satisfied, to satisfy	múhnjūk	滿足
Saturday	Sīngkèih-luhk/Láihbaai-luhk	星期六 / 禮拜六
sauce	jāp	汁
sauce (chilli)	laahtjīu-jeung	辣椒醬
say, to	góng	講
say hello	mahnhauh	問候
say goodbye	douhbiht	道別
say sorry	douhhip	道歉
say thankyou	douhjeh	道謝
scales	ching/bóng*	秤 / 磅
scarce	kyutfaht	缺乏
scared	pa	怕
scenery	jihyìhn fūnggíng	自然風景
schedule	sìhgaan-bíu/yahtchìhng-bíu	時間表 / 日程表
school	hohkhaauh	學校
scissors	gaaujín	較剪
Scotland	Sōugaaklàahn	蘇格蘭
Scottish (in general)	Sōugaaklàahn ge	蘇格蘭嘅
Scottish, Scots	Sōugaaklàahn-yàhn	蘇格蘭人
screw-driver	lòhsīpāi	螺絲批
sea	hói	海
seafood	hóisīn	海鮮
search for, to	wáhn	搵
season	gwaijit	季節
seat	johwái*	座位
second (in sequence)	daihyih	第二
secret	beimaht	秘密
secretary	bei'syū	秘書
secure, safe	ngōnchyùhn	安全
see, to	tái-gin	睇見
seed	júngjí	種子
seek, to	chàhmkàuh	尋求
seem, to	chíhfùh	似乎
see you later!	yātjahn gin	一陣見
seldom	hóusíu	好少
select, to	gáan	揀
self	jihgéi	自己
sell, to	maaih	賣
send, to	sung	送
sensible	hahp-chìhngléih / mìhngji	合情理 / 明智
sentence	geui	句
separate (couple, lovers)	fānsáu	分手

separate, to	fān-hōi	分開
September	Gáu-yuht	九月
sequence, order	chijeuih	次序
serious (not funny)	yìhmsūk	嚴肅
serious (severe)	yìhmjuhng	嚴重
servant	gūngyàhn	工人
service	fuhkmouh	服務
sesame oil	màhyàuh	麻油
seven	chāt	七
seventeen	sahp-chāt	十七
seventy	chāt-sahp	七十
several	géi (go)	幾（個）
severe	yìhmlaih	嚴厲
sex, gender	singbiht	性別
sex, sexual activity	jouh'ngoi/oi	做愛
shall, will	jēungyiu	將要
shallow	chín	淺
shame, disgrace	cháu/sāugā	醜／羞家
shame: what a shame!	jānhaih hósīk!	真係可惜!
shampoo	sáitàuh-séui	洗頭水
Shanghai	Seuhnghói	上海
shape	yìhngjohng	形狀
shark	sāyùh	鯊魚
sharp	leih	利
she, her	kéuih	佢
sheet (for bed)	chòhngdāan	床單
ship	syùhn	船
shirt	sēut'sāam	恤衫
shit	sí	屎
shiver, to	dá-láahngjan	打冷震
shoes	hàaih	鞋
shop, store	poutáu*	舖頭
shop, go shopping	máaih-yéh	買嘢
short (concise)	dyún	短
short (not tall)	ngái	矮
shorts (short trousers)	dyúnfu	短褲
shorts (underpants)	dáifu	底褲
shoulder	boktàuh	膊頭
shout, to	daaihsēng ngaai	大聲嗌
show (live performance)	bíuyín	表演
show, to	béi yàhn tái	俾人睇
shower (for washing)	fāsá	花洒
shower (of rain)	jaauh'yúh	驟雨
shower, to take a	chūng-fāsá	沖花洒
shrimp, prawn	saihā	細蝦
shut	sāan	門
sibling	hīngdaih-jímuih	兄弟姊妹
sick, ill	behng-jó	病咗
sick to be (vomit)	ngáutou	嘔吐
side	pòhngbīn	旁邊
sightseeing	tái-fūnggíng	睇風景
sign, road	louhpáai*	路牌
signature, to sign	chīmméng*	簽名
silent	jihng	靜
silk	sīchàuh	絲綢
silver	ngàhn	銀
similar	sēungchíh	相似
simple (easy)	yùhngyih	容易
simple (uncomplicated)	gáandāan	簡單

since	jihchùhng	自從
sing, to	cheung-gō	唱歌
Singapore	Sān'gabō	新加坡
Singaporean (in general)	Sān'gabō ge	新加坡嘅
Singaporean (people)	Sān'gabō-yàhn	新加坡人
single (not married)	dāansān	單身
single (only one)	yāt go yàhn	一個人
sir (term of address)	sīnsāang	先生
sister (older)	jèhjē*	姐姐
sister (younger)	mùihmúi*	妹妹
sit, to	chóh	坐
sit down, to	chóh-dāi	坐低
situation, how things are	chìhngfong	情況
six	luhk	六
sixteen	sahp-luhk	十六
sixty	luhk-sahp	六十
size	daaihsai	大細
skewer	chyunsīu	串燒
skilful	suhklihn	熟練
skin	pèihfū	皮膚
skirt	kwàhn	裙
sky	tīnhūng	天空
sleep, to	fan'gaau	瞓覺
sleepy	ngáahnfan	眼瞓
slender	saichèuhng	細長
slightly	sáauwàih	稍為
slim	míuhtíuh	苗條
slippers	tōháai*	拖鞋
slope	sāanbō	山坡
slow	maahn	慢
slowly	maahnmáan*déi*	慢慢地
small	sai	細
smart	chūngmìhng	聰明
smell, bad odor	chaumeih	臭味
smell, to	màhn	聞
smile, to	siu	笑
smoke	yīn	煙
smoke, to (tobacco)	sihk-yīn	食煙
smooth (unproblematic)	seuhnleih	順利
smooth (of surfaces)	pìhng'waaht	平滑
smuggle, to (illegal goods)	jáausī	走私
snake	sèh	蛇
sneeze, to	dá-hātchī	打乞嗤
snow	syut	雪
snow, to	lohk-syut	落雪
snowpeas	hòhlāan-dáu*	荷蘭豆
so (degree)	gám*yéung*	咁樣
so, therefore	sóyíh	所以
soap	fāan'gáan	番硯
soccer	jūkkàuh	足球
socket (electric)	chaaptàuh	插頭
socks	maht	襪
sofa, couch	sōfá*	梳化
soft	yúhn	軟
soft drink	heiséui	汽水
sold	maaih-jó	賣咗
soldier	sihbīng	士兵
sold out	maaih-saai	賣晒
sole, only	wàihyāt	唯一

solve, to (a problem)	gáai'kyut	解決
some	yāt-dī	一啲
somebody, someone	yáuhyàhn	有人
something	(yáuh-dī) yéh	(有啲) 嘢
sometimes	yáuhsìh	有時
somewhere	máuh'chyu	某處
son	jái	仔
son-in-law	néuihsai	女婿
song	gō(kūk)	歌（曲）
soon	(jauh) faai	（就）快
sore, painful	tung	痛
sorry, to feel regretful	hauhfui	後悔
sorry!	deui'm̀h-jyuh	對唔住
sort, type	júngleuih	種類
sort out, deal with	gáai'kyut	解決
sound, noise	sēngyām	聲音
sour	syūn	酸
source	lòih'yùhn	來源
south	nàahm'bīn/bihn	南邊
south-east	dūng'nàahm	東南
south-west	sāi'nàahm	西南
souvenir	géi'nihmbán	紀念品
soy sauce	sāangchāu	生抽
spacious	futlohk	闊落
speak, to	góng	講
special	dahkbiht	特別
spectacles	ngáahn'géng*	眼鏡
speech, to make a speech	yín'góng	演講
speed	chūkdouh	速度
spell, to	chyun	串
spend, to	sái-chín*	洗錢
spices	hēunglíu*	香料
spinach	bōchoi	菠菜
spine	buijek-gwāt	背脊骨
spoiled (of children)	jungwaaih-jó	縱壞咗
spoiled (of food)	waaih-jó / sūk-jó	壞咗／嗕咗
spoon	chìhgāng	匙羹
sports	wahnduhng	運動
spring (season)	chēuntīn	春天
spring (of water)	kwongchyùhn-séui	礦泉水
spouse	pui'ngáuh	配偶
square (shape)	jingfōng-yìhng	正方形
square, town square	gwóngchèuhng	廣場
stain	wūdím	污點
stairs	làuhtāi	樓梯
stall (of vendor)	tāan	攤
stall, to (car)	séifó	死火
stamp (postage)	yàuhpiu	郵票
stand, to	kéih	企
stand up, to	kéih-héisān	企起身
star	sīng	星
start, beginning	hōichí	開始
start, to	faatduhng	發動
stationery	màhn'geuih	文具
stay overnight, to	gwo-yé*	過夜
steal, to	tāu	偷
steamed	jīng ge	蒸嘅
steel	gong	鋼
step	bouh	步

steps, stairs	làuhtāi-kāp	樓梯級
sticky	chī-nahp-nahp	黐笠笠
stiff	ngaahng	硬
still, quiet	pìhngjihng	平靜
stink, to	faatchau	發臭
stomach, belly	tóuh	肚
stone	sehktàuh	石頭
stool/chair	dang	凳
stop (bus, train)	jaahm	站
stop, to	tìhng	停
store, shop	poutáu*	舖頭
store, to	chyúhchòhng	儲藏
storm	dáfūng	打風
story (of a building)	chàhng/láu*	層／樓
story (tale)	gú*jái	故仔
stove, cooker	lòuhtàuh	爐頭
straight (not crooked)	jihk	直
straight ahead	yātjihk heui	一直去
strange	kèihgwaai	奇怪
stranger	sāangbóu*-yàhn	生步人
street	gāai	街
strength	lihk	力
strict	yìhm'gaak	嚴格
strike, hit	dá	打
string	síng	繩
strong	kèuhngjong	強壯
stubborn, determined	ngaahng'géng	硬頸
student	hohksāang	學生
study, learn	hohk	學
stupid	bahn/chéun	笨／蠢
style	fūnggaak	風格
succeed, to (follow)	gaisìhng	繼承
success	sìhnggūng	成功
such	gámyéung*	噉樣
such as, for example	laihyùh	例如
suddenly	dahkyìhn	突然
sugar	tòhng	糖
suggestion, to suggest	tàihyíh	提議
suit, business	sāijōng	西裝
suitable, fitting	ngāamsān	啱身
suitcase	pèihgīp	皮夾
summer	hahtīn	夏天
summit, peak	sāanténg*	山頂
sun	taaiyèuhng	太陽
Sunday	Sīngkèih-yaht/Láihbaai-yaht	星期日／禮拜日
sunlight	yèuhnggwōng	陽光
sunscreen lotion	taaiyèuhng-yàuh/ fòhngsaai-yàuh	太陽油／防晒油
sunny	chìhnglóhng	晴朗
sunrise	yahtchēut	日出
sunset	yahtlohk	日落
supermarket	chīukāp-síhchèuhng	超級市場
suppose, to	gádihng	假定
sure	hángdihng/kokdihng	肯定／確定
surface	bíumihn	表面
surface mail	pìhngyàuh	平郵
surname	sing	姓
surprised	gīngkèih / gám-dou yi'ngoih	驚奇／感到意外
surprising	lihng yàhn gám-dou yi'ngoih	令人感到意外

surroundings	wàahn'gíng	環境
survive, to	sāngchyùhn	生存
suspect, to	wàaihyìh	懷疑
swallow, to	tān	吞
sweat	hohn	汗
sweat, to	chēut-hohn	出汗
sweet (taste)	tìhm	甜
sweet, dessert	tìhmbán	甜品
sweet and sour	tìhmsyūn	甜酸
sweetcorn	sūkmáih	粟米
sweets, candy	tóng*	糖
swim, to	yàuhséui	游水
swimming costume	wihngyī	泳衣
swimming pool	yàuhwihng-chìh	游泳池
switch	jai	掣
synthetic	yàhnjouh ge	人造嘅

T

table	tói	檯
tablecloth	tóibou	檯布
tablets	yeuhk'yún	藥丸
tail	méih	尾
take, to remove	ló-jáu	攞走
take care of, to	fuhjaak	負責
talk, to	kīnggái	傾偈
tall	gōu	高
Taoism	Douhgaau	道教
tape, adhesive	gāaují	膠紙
tape, recording	luhkyām-dáai*	錄音帶
taste	meihdouh	味道
taste, to (sample)	sī	試
taste, to (salty, spicy)	si-meih	試味
tasty	hóusihk	好食
taxi	dīksí	的士
tea	chàh	茶
teach, to	gaau	教
teacher	gaausī	教師
tears	ngáahnleuih	眼淚
teenager	chīngsiu'nìhn	青少年
teeshirt	tīsēut	T恤
teeth	ngàh	牙
telephone	dihnwá*	電話
telephone number	dihnwá* houhmáh	電話號碼
television	dihnsih	電視
tell, to (a story)	góng	講
tell, to (let ... know)	wah béi ... jī	話俾 ... 知
temperature (heat)	wāndouh	溫度
temperature (body)	táiwān	體溫
temple (Chinese)	míu*	廟
temporary	jaahm'sìh	暫時
ten	sahp	十
ten million	chīn-maahn	千萬
tennis	móhngkàuh	網球
tens of, multiples of ten	géi-sahp	幾十
tense	gánjēung	緊張
ten thousand	maahn	萬
terrible	hópa	可怕
test	siyihm	試驗
test, to	chāakyihm	測驗

testicles	gōuyún	睾丸
Thai (in general)	Taaigwok ge	泰國嘅
Thai (language)	Taaimán*	泰文
Thai (people)	Taaigwok-yàhn	泰國人
Thailand	Taaigwok	泰國
thankyou, to thank	m̀h'gōi/dōjeh	唔該 / 多謝
that, those	gó	嗰
theater (drama)	kehk'yún	劇院
their, theirs	kéuihdeih ge	佢哋嘅
then	yìhnhauh	然後
there	gódouh/gósyu	嗰度 / 嗰處
therefore	yānchí	因此
there is, there are	yáuh	有
these	nīdī	呢啲
they, them	kéuihdeih	佢哋
thick (of liquids)	nùhng	濃
thick (of things)	háuh	厚
thief	cháak*/síutāu	賊 / 小偷
thigh	daaihtéui	大腿
thin (of liquids)	hēi	稀
thin (of persons)	sau	瘦
thing	yéh	嘢
think, to ponder	séung/háauleuih	想 / 考慮
think, to have an opinion	yihng'wàih	認為
third (in a series)	daihsāam	第三
third (1/3)	sāamfahnjī-yāt	三分之一
thirsty	háu'hot	口渴
thirty	sāam-sahp	三十
this	nī	呢
though	sēuiyìhn	雖然
thoughts	séungfaat	想法
thousand	chīn	千
thread	sin	線
threaten, to	húnghaak	恐嚇
three	sāam	三
throat	hàuhlùhng	喉嚨
through, past	tūnggwo	通過
throw, to	dám	揼
throw away, throw out	dám-jó	揼咗
thunder	dálèuih	打雷
Thursday	Sīngkèih-sei/Láihbaai-sei	星期四 / 禮拜四
thus, so	yūsih	於是
ticket	fēi/piu	飛 / 票
tidy	jíngchàih	整齊
tidy up	sāusahp	收拾
tie, necktie	léhngtāai	領呔
tie, to	bóng	綁
tiger	lóuhfú	老虎
tight	gán	緊
time	sìhgaan	時間
time: from time to time	gaanjūng	間中
timetable	sìhgaan-bíu	時間表
tiny	saisíu	細小
tip (gratuity)	tīpsí	貼士
tired (sleepy)	ngáahnfan	眼瞓
tired (worn out)	gwuih	癐
title (of book, film)	bīutàih	標題
title (of person)	hàahmtàuh	銜頭
to, toward	heung/deui	向 / 對

toasted	hong	烘
today	gāmyaht	今日
toe	geukjí	腳趾
tofu	dauhfuh	豆腐
together	yātchàih	一齊
toilet	chisó / sáisáu-gāan	廁所 / 洗手間
tomato	fāanké	蕃茄
tomorrow	tīngyaht	聽日
tongue	leih	脷
tonight	gāmmáahn	今晚
too (also)	dōuhaih	都係
too (excessive)	taai	太
too much	taai dō	太多
tool	gūnggeuih	工具
tooth	ngàh	牙
toothbrush	ngàhcháat*	牙刷
toothpaste	ngàhgōu	牙膏
top	déng*	頂
topic	tàihmuhk	題目
torch, flashlight	dihntúng	電筒
total	yātguhng	一共
touch, to	mó	摸
tourist	léuihhaak/yàuhhaak	旅客 / 遊客
toward (people/place)	heung	向
towel	mòuhgan	毛巾
tower	taap	塔
town	síhjan	市鎮
toy	wuhn'geuih	玩具
trade, to exchange	gāauyihk	交易
traditional	chyùhntúng	傳統
traffic	gāautūng	交通
train	fóchē	火車
train station	fóchē-jaahm	火車站
training	fanlihn	訓練
translate, to	fāanyihk	翻譯
travel, to	léuihhàhng	旅行
traveler	léuihhaak	旅客
tray	tokpún*	托盤
treat (something special)	tìhm'táu*	甜頭
treat, to (behave towards)	deui-yàhn	對人
treat, to (medically)	yī	醫
tree	syuh	樹
triangle	sāamgok-yìhng	三角形
trip, journey	léuihhàhng/léuihchìhng	旅行 / 旅程
troops	gwāndéui*	軍隊
trouble, troublesome	màhfàahn	麻煩
trousers	fu	褲
truck	fóchē	火車
true	jān	真
trust, to	seunyahm	信任
try, to	si	試
try on (clothes)	sisān	試身
Tuesday	Sīngkèih-yih/Láihbaai-yih	星期二 / 禮拜二
turn around, to	jyun	轉
turn off, to	sāan/sīk	門 / 熄
turn on, to	hōi	開
TV	dihnsih-gēi	電視機
twelve	sahp-yih	十二
twenty	yih-sahp	二十

twice	léuhng chi	兩次
two (numeral)	yih	二
two (measure)	léuhng	兩
type, sort	júngleuih	種類
type, to	dájih	打字
typhoon	dáfūng	打風
typical	dínyìhng	典型

U

ugly	cháuyéung*	醜樣
umbrella	jē	遮
under	hahmihn	下面
undergo, to	gīnggwo	經過
underpants	dáifu	底褲
undershirt	dáisāam	底衫
understand	mìhng	明
unfortunately	m̀h'hóuchói	唔好彩
unemployed	sātyihp	失業
unhappy	m̀h'hōisām	唔開心
United Kingdom	Yīnggwok	英國
United States	Méihgwok	美國
university	daaihhohk	大學
unleaded petrol	mòuh'yùhn-dihnyàuh	無鉛電油
unless	chèuihfēi	除非
unlucky	dóumùih	倒霉
until	jihkdou	直到
up, upward	heungseuhng	向上
upset, unhappy	m̀h'hōisām	唔開心
upstairs	làuhseuhng	樓上
urban	sìhngsíh	城市
urgent	gán'gāp	緊急
urinate, to	síubihn	小便
us	ngóhdeih	我哋
use, to	yuhng	用
used to	jaahpgwaan	習慣
useful	yáuhyuhng ge	有用嘅
useless	móuhyuhng ge	冇用嘅
usually	tūngsèuhng	通常

V

vacation	gakèih	假期
vaccination	dá-fòhngyihk-jām	打防疫針
vagina	yāmdouh	陰道
vague	hàhm'wùh	含糊
valid	yáuhhaauh	有效
value (cost)	gajihk	價值
value, good	jihkdāk	值得
value, to	juhngsih	重視
VCR	luhkyíng-gēi	錄影機
vegetable	sōchoi	蔬菜
vegetarian	sihk-jāai	食齋
vehicle	chē	車
via	louhgīng	路經
video recorder	sipluhk-gēi	攝錄機
Vietnam	Yuht'nàahm	越南
Vietnamese (in general)	Yuht'nàahm ge	越南嘅
Vietnamese (people)	Yuht'nàahm-yàhn	越南人
Vietnamese (language)	Yuht'nàahm-wá*	越南話
view, panorama	fūnggíng	風景

view, look at	tái	睇
village	chyūn	村
vinegar	chou	醋
visa	chīmjing	簽証
visit	chāam'gwūn	參觀
visit, to pay a	fóngmahn	訪問
voice	sēngyām	聲音
voicemail	dihnwá* làuhyìhn	電話留言
vomit, to	ngáu	嘔
vote, to	tàuh-piu	投票

W

wages	yàhn'gūng	人工
wait for, to	dáng	等
waiter, waitress	sihying-sāng	侍應生
wake up	séng*	醒
wake someone up	giu-séng*	叫醒
Wales	Wāiyíhsī	威爾斯
walk, to	hàahng	行
walking distance	hàahng-dāk-dou	行得到
wall	chèuhng	墙
wallet	ngàhnbāau	銀包
want, to	yiu	要
war, to make	dá-jeung	打仗
warm, warmth	nyúhn	暖
warning, to warn	gínggou	警告
wash, to	sái	洗
wash the dishes	sái-wún	洗碗
watch (wristwatch)	sáubīu	手錶
watch, to	tái	睇
watch over, guard	hōn-jyuh	看住
water	séui	水
waterfall	buhkbou	瀑布
watermelon	sāi'gwā	西瓜
wave (in sea)	lohng	浪
wave, to	jīusáu	招手
way, method	fōngfaat	方法
way: by way of	louhging	路徑
way in	yahp'háu	入口
way out	chēutháu	出口
we, us	ngóhdeih	我哋
weak	yeuhk	弱
wealthy	yáuhchín*	有錢
wear, to	jeuk	著
weary	gwuih	癐
weather	tīnhei	天氣
wedding	fānláih	婚禮
Wednesday	Sīngkèih-sāam/ Láihbaai-sāam	星期三／禮拜三
week	sīngkèih/láihbaai	星期
weekend	jāumuht	週末
weekly	múih go sīngkèih/láihbaai	每個星期／禮拜
weep, to	haam	喊
weigh, to	ching/bong*	秤／磅
weigh out, to	ching-chēut	秤出
weight	chúhngleuhng	重量
weight (body)	táichúhng	體重
weight, to gain	jāng-bóng*	增磅
weight, to lose	gáam-bóng*/gáam-fèih	減磅／減肥

welcome! , welcome, to	fūnyìhng	歡迎
well (good)	hóu	好
well-cooked, well-done	jyú-tau	煮透
well done!	jouh-dāk hóu	做得好
well-mannered	yáuh-láihmaauh	有禮貌
well off, wealthy	yáuhchín*	有錢
Welsh (in general)	Wāiyíhsī ge	威爾斯嘅
Welsh (people)	Wāiyíhsī-yàhn	威爾斯人
west	sāi'bīn/bihn	西邊
Westerner	Sāiyàhn	西人
wet	sāp	濕
what	mātyéh	乜嘢
what for	dímgáai	點解
what kind of	bīn júng	邊種
what time	géidím	幾點
wheel	chēlūk	車轆
when	géisìh	幾時
when, at the time	dōng / ... ge sìhhauh	當 / ...嘅時候
whenever	mòuhleuhn hòhsìh	無論何時
where	bīndouh/bīnsyu	邊度 / 邊處
where to	heui bīn'douh/heui bīnsyu	去邊度 / 去邊處
which one	bīn (go)	邊 (個)
while, during	hái/héung ... kèihgāan	喺 / 響 ... 期間
white	baahksīk	白色
who	bīn'go/bīnwái*	邊個 / 邊位
whole, all of	chyùhnbouh	全部
whole, to be complete	jíng go	整個
why?	dímgáai	點解
wicked	waaih sāmchèuhng ge	壞心腸嘅
wide	fut	闊
width	futdouh	闊度
widow	gwáfúh	寡婦
widowed	yíh-song'ngáuh	已喪偶
widower	gwāanfū	鰥夫
wife	taaitáai*/lóuhpòh	太太 / 老婆
wild	yéhsāng ge	野生嘅
will, shall	(jēung) wúih	(將) 會
win, to	yèhng	贏
wind, breeze	fūng	風
window (in house)	chēung	窗
window (for paying, buying tickets)	chēungháu	窗口
wine	pòuhtòuh-jáu	葡萄酒
winner	dākjéung-yàhn	得獎人
winter	dūngtīn	冬天
wipe, to	maat-gōn	抹乾
wise	chūngmìhng	聰明
wish, to	hēimohng	希望
with, and	tùhng	同
within reason	chìhngléih jī'noih	情理之內
without	móuh	冇
witness	jingyàhn	証人
witness, to	chān'ngáahn gin-dóu*	親眼見到
woman	néuihyán*	女人
wonderful	hóugihk laak	好極嘞
wood	muhktàuh	木頭
wooden	muhkjai ge	木製嘅
wool	yèuhngmòuh/lāang	羊毛 / 冷
wool (for knitting)	lāang	冷

work	gūngjok	工作
work, to	jouh	做
work, to function	héi-jokyuhng	起作用
world	saigaai	世界
worn out, tired	gwuih	攰
worn out (clothes, machine)	chàhn'gaau	陳舊
worry, to	dāamsām	擔心
worse	gang'waaih/gang chā	更壞／更差
worst	jeui'waaih/jeui chā	最壞／最差
worth, to be	jihkdāk	值得
wound	sēungháu	傷口
wrap, to	bāau	包
wrist	sáuwún	手腕
write, to	sé	寫
writer	jokgā	作家
wrong (false)	m̀h'ngāam	唔啱
wrong (mistaken)	cho	錯
wrong (morally)	bāt-douhdāk	不道德

Y

yawn	dá-haamlouh	打喊路
year	nìhn	年
years old	seui	歲
yell, to	daaihsēng giu	大聲叫
yellow	wòhng	黃
yes	haih	係
yesterday	kàhm/chàhm'yaht	琴／尋日
yet: not yet	juhng meih	仲未
you	néih	你
you (plural)	néihdeih	你哋
you're welcome!	m̀h'sái haakhei	唔駛客氣
young	hauhsāang / nìhnhēng	後生／年輕
youth (state of being young)	chīngchēun	青春
youth (young person)	hauhsāangjái'néui*	後生仔女

Z

| zero | lìhng | 零 |
| zoo | duhngmaht-yùhn | 動物園 |

Basic Grammar

Compared to many European languages, Cantonese grammar is quite simple. There are no verb conjugations, no plurals, no gender in nouns, no articles and the sentence order is intuitive to English speakers. The following is an outline of Cantonese grammar using parts of speech familiar to English speakers.

Word Order

More often than not, Cantonese word order is the same as in English:

subject — verb — object

Ngóh hohk Gwóngdūng-wá*　我學廣東話。　'I study Cantonese.'

Nouns and Pronouns

Cantonese words are mostly made up of one or two characters and nouns are no different. No distinction is made between singular and plural nouns. When it is necessary to distinguish plurals, this is done through the use of measure words which indicate the number of items involved. For example, the word for 'hotel', jáudim can be either singular or plural unless it is necessary to indicate that there are more than one. Thus,

yāt gāan jáudim	一間酒店	'one hotel'
léuhng gāan jáudim	兩間酒店	'two hotels'
sāam gāan jáudim	三間酒店	'three hotels'

In the above examples, the noun jáudim 酒店 'hotel' is qualified by a number with the appropriate measure word gāan 間 which indicates whether or not it is singular or plural. You will notice that whereas the number yih 二 'two' is used in counting, e.g. Yāt yih sāam ... 一二三...'one, two, three ...' the word léuhng 兩 'a couple of' replaces yih 'two' where a measure word is used.

Like nouns, Cantonese personal pronouns do not change form whether they are used as subjects or objects. Simple personal pronouns are: ngóh 我 'I/me', néih 你 'you', kéuih 佢 'he/him/she/her/it' (the last two pronouns share the same pronunciation but are written with different characters).

Unlike nouns, however, Cantonese personal pronouns can take on plural forms with the addition of the vernacular suffix -deih 哋, making the above examples into ngóhdeih 我哋 'we/us', néihdeih 你哋 'you (plural)', kéuihdeih 佢哋 'they/them' (also used for animals or insects). Another suffix -mùhn 們 replaces -deih 哋 in formal instances involving the first and second person, ngóh 我 'I/me' and néih 你 'you', giving the compounds ngóhmùhn 我們 'we/us' and néihmùhn 你們 'you (plural)'. This formal suffix -mùhn 們 can also be added to nouns in greetings, e.g. néuihsihmùhn, sīnsāangmùhn 女士們，先生們 'ladies and gentlemen'. The usage of putting a suffix after a noun is applied sparingly as it is unnecessary to indicate plural forms in Cantonese nouns.

In addition to personal pronouns, there are demonstrative pronouns, for example, nī 呢 'this' and gó 嗰 'that'. It is important to note that a plural measure word dī 啲 is added to give the plural forms of these pronouns: nīdī 呢啲 'these', gódī 嗰啲 'those' and bīndī 邊啲 'which ones', but it is not a plural form in the sense that -mùhn is used.

Possessives and Measure words

To make a possessive out of a noun or pronoun, simply add the particle ge 嘅. Thus 'the tour guide's', 'Miss Li's', 'my/mine', 'your/yours', 'his/her' become: douhyàuh ge 導遊嘅, Léih síujé ge 李小姐嘅, ngóh ge 我嘅, néih ge 你嘅, kéuih ge 佢嘅, ngóhdeih ge 我哋 嘅, néihdeih ge 你哋嘅, kéuihdeih ge 佢哋嘅, etc.

You have learnt to use measure words in conjunction with numbers to indicate the plural form of a noun. In English we say 'a slice/loaf of bread', 'a piece/ream of paper', 'a school of fish' etc. In Cantonese this usage applies to all nouns in order to specify number, e.g. 'a book' is yāt bún syū 一本書, 'a table' is yāt jēung tói 一張檯, and 'two chairs' is léuhng jēung dang 兩張凳 etc. As you can see from the above examples, there isn't one unique measure word for each noun. In fact, measure words tend to describe classes of objects with similar characteristics. Thus the word bún 本 describes bound books, jēung 張 describes wide, flat objects of many types such as tables, paper, bedsheets etc., even chairs, and bá 把 describes things with handles including knives, forks etc. Luckily for beginners of the language, there is a general-use measure word go 個 which is used in simple phrases like nī go 呢個 'this one', gó go 嗰個 'that one', bīn go 邊個 'which one' or géi go 幾個 'several' or 'how many (items)'?

Verbs

Cantonese verbs are not conjugated, but keep one simple form regardless of the subject or tense. Thus the verb sihk 食 'eat' is the same whether the subject is I, you, he/she or they, and whether the action took place yesterday or will happen two days from now. However, there are ways to indicate tense in Chinese sentences, e.g. the use of time words before the verb, the use of the particles gwo 過 and jó 咗 to indicate past and completed action, and the use of jauh 就 and wúih 會 to indicate future action. For example,

The use of time words before the verb:

Ngóh kàhmyaht sihk yú*.	我琴日食魚。	'Yesterday I ate fish.'
Ngóh gāmyaht sihk yú*.	我今日食魚。	'Today I eat fish.'
Ngóh tīngyaht sihk yú*.	我聽日食魚。	'Tomorrow I'll be eating fish.'

Note that the Cantonese verb sihk 食 'eat' does not change to indicate tense, this is done through the use of kàhmyaht 琴日 'yesterday', gāmyaht 今日 'today' and tīngyaht 聽日 'tomorrow'.

The particle gwo 過 is used after the verb to indicate an action that occurred in an unspecified time in the past:

Ngóh sihk-gwo yú.	我食過魚。	'I've eaten fish previously.'

The use of the particle jó 咗 after the verb indicates that the action has just been recently completed:

Ngóh sihk-jó yú.	我食咗魚。	'I've just eaten (the) fish.'

The use of the aspect partices jauh 就 'soon' or wúih 會 'will/shall' before the verb to indicate future action:

Ngóh jauh sihk yú.	我就食喇啲魚。	'I'm going to eat (the) fish.'
Ngóh wúih sihk gódī yú.	我會食喇啲魚。	'I'll be eating (the) fish.'

Adjectives

Adjectives in Cantonese are simple as they don't need to agree in gender or number with the nouns they modify. They are sometimes called stative verbs as they incorporate the verb 'to be' in the sentence. In its positive form, adjectives are generally preceded by the adverb hóu 好 'very'. Thus, Ngóh hóu gōuhing 我好高興 means 'I'm very happy.'

When adjectives modify nouns in phrases they generally precede the noun, often using the particle ge 嘅 in between. Where an adjective has a single syllable, the use of the particle ge 嘅 is omitted. For example,

sīn cháangjāp	鮮橙汁	'gresh orange juice'
hāk gafē	黑咖啡	'black coffee'
màihyàhn ge fūnggíng	迷人嘅風景	'enchanting scenery'
mìhnggwai ge láihmaht	名貴嘅禮物	'expensive gift'
tóuyim ge wūyīng	討厭嘅烏蠅	'annoying flies'

Adverbs

Just as adjectives precede the nouns they modify, adverbs are placed before verbs, adjectives or other adverbs to express time, degree, scope, repetition, possibility, negotiation and tone of speech. Common examples are: hóu 好 'very', dōu 都 'also', béigaau 比較 'rather', jauh 就 'then', sèhngyaht 成日 'always'. For example,

Nī tìuh louh hóu chèuhng.	呢條路好長。	'This road is very long.'
Ngóh dōu séung máaih.	我都想買。	'I'm also thinking of buying.'
Nīdouh hahtīn béigaau yiht.	呢度夏天比較熱。	'The summer here is quite hot.'
Néih heui sīn, ngóh jauh làih.	你先去, 我就嚟。	'Go first, I'll catch up with you.'
Nīdouh sèhngyaht lohkyúh.	呢度成日落雨。	'It is always raining here.'

Negatives

There are generally two particles that are used for forming the negative in Cantonese: m̀h and móuh 冇. The former is placed before verbs or adjectives to indicate negation in simple present tense while the latter is used to indicate negation of an action that happened in the past. For example:

| Seuhnghói dūngtīn m̀h`lohksyut. | 上海冬天唔落雪。 | 'It does not snow in Shanghai in winter.' |
| Gauhnín* Bākgīng móuh lohksyut. | 舊年北京冇落雪。 | 'Last year it didn't snow in Beijing.' |

Interrogatives

There are three basic ways to ask questions in Cantonese. The most common way is to add the particle ma 嗎 at the end of a declarative sentence.

| Néih ngoh ma? | 你餓嗎? | 'Are you hungry?' |
| Néih hōisām ma? | 你開心嗎? | 'Are you happy?' |

The second way is to use the choice-type question which presents the listener with two opposite alternatives.

| Néih ngoh-m̀h-ngoh a? | 你餓唔餓呀? | 'Are you hungry?' |
| Néih hōi-m̀h-hōisām ma? | 你開唔開心呀? | 'Are you happy?' |

The third way is by using an interrogative pronoun. Examples are: bīnwái* 邊位 'who', mātyéh 乜嘢 'what', dímyéung* 點樣 'how', bīn + MW (邊 + measure word) / 邊啲 'which', bīndouh/bīnsyu 邊度 / 邊處 'where', dímgáai 點解 'why', géidím/géisìh 幾點 / 幾時 'when'.

1. Néih haih bīnwái* a?	你係邊位呀?	'Who are you?'
2. Néih giujouh mātyéh méng* a?	你叫做乜嘢名呀?	'What's your name?'
3. Néih dímyéung* yahp-làih ga?	你點樣入嚟㗎?	'How did you get in?'
4. Néih hái bīn'go mùhnháu yahp-làih ga?	你喺邊個門口入嚟㗎?	'Which door did you get in?'

5. Néih bàhbā màhmā hái bīndouh a?	你爸爸媽媽喺邊度呀？	'Where are your parents?'
6. Néih dímgáai m̀h'chēut-sēng a?	你點解唔出聲呀？	'Why aren't you saying anything?'
7. Yìhgā géidím la?	而家幾點喇？	'What's the time now?'
8. Néih géisìh yahp-làih ga?	你幾時入嚟㗎？	'When did you come here?'

In answering a question involving the interrogative pronoun, follow the grammar of the question and note its word order, changing the subject of the sentence where appropriate, e.g. néih 你 'you' becomes ngóh 我 'I' when you answer a question. Then, just substitute the noun which gives the information with the interrogative pronoun. For example, when you asked the lost child who wandered into your room using the above questions, the anwers to some of your questions may be:

1. Ngóh haih Asām.	我係阿森。	'I'm Ah Sum.'
2. Ngóh giujouh Asām.	我叫做阿森。	'I'm called Ah Sum.'
3. Ngóh dohngsāt-jó-louh.	我蕩失咗路。	'I'm lost.'
4. Ngóh hái gó go mùhnháu yahp-làih ge.	我喺嗰個門口入嚟㗎。	'I came in from that door.'
5. Ngóh bàhbā màhmā hái jáudim.	我爸爸媽媽喺酒店。	'They are in the hotel.'
6. Ngóh dohngsāt-jó-louh, ngóh pa.	我蕩失咗路，我怕。	'I'm lost, I'm scared.'
7. Ngóh m̀h'jī yìhgā géidím jūng.	我唔知而家幾點鐘。	'I don't know the time.'
8. Ngóh yahp-jó-làih hóu noih la.	我入咗嚟好耐喇。	'I've been here a long time.'

Yes/No answers

For questions ending with the interrogative particle ma 嗎, take away the question particle, and answer according to the situation that you find yourself in. There are no specific words in Chinese for 'yes' and 'no'. The closest equivalent is haih 係 and m̀h'haih 唔係, respectively. Usually, when a Cantonese speaker is asked a question, they will repeat the verb used in the question to answer in the affirmative. If they want to answer in the negative, they add the negation word m̀h 唔 before the verb in the sentence. Similarly, for choice-type question the opposite alternatives can be either 'yes' or 'no'. Thus,

'Yes' answer: hóu ngoh	好餓。	'Yes, I'm very hungry.'
'No' answer: m̀h'ngoh	唔餓。	'No, I'm not hungry.'
'Yes' answer: hōisām.	開心。	'Yes, I'm happy.'
'No' answer: m̀h'hōisām	唔開心。	'No, I'm not happy.'